By the Seats of their Pants

Terry Gwynn-Jones was born in England. He served as a fighter pilot and jet instructor with the British, Canadian and Australian air forces before joining Australia's Department of Civil Aviation in 1969 as an Examiner of Airmen. In 1975, with another ex-RAF pilot, he set an around-the-world speed record for piston-engined aircraft. In 1988, he gave up flying to pursue a full-time writing career.

Since 1972 he has published twelve books and hundreds of magazine articles. He was a consultant and writer for Time-Life's *Epic of Flight* and *How Things Work* series. Following resident writing assignments with the Smithsonian Institution's National Air & Space Museum, he was appointed to the Board of Advisors of the Smithsonian Institution's History of Aviation book project. His first collection of great Australian air stories, *On a Wing and a Prayer*, was published by UQP in 1989. In 1991 his most recent books, *Wings Across the Pacific, Farther & Faster* and *How Things Work — Flight* were published in Australia and the USA.

By the Seats of their Pants

more great Australian air stories

TERRY GWYNN-JONES

University of Queensland Press

First published 1992 by University of Queensland Press
Box 42, St Lucia, Queensland 4067 Australia

Typeset by University of Queensland Press
Printed in Australia by The Book Printer, Victoria

Distributed in the USA and Canada by
International Specialized Book Services, Inc.,
5602 N.E. Hassalo Street, Portland, Oregon 97213-3640

Cataloguing in Publication Data
National Library of Australia

Gwynn-Jones, Terry, 1933-
     By the seat of their pants : more great Australian air
     stories.

     Bibliography.
     Includes index.

     1. Air pilots – Australia – Biography. 2. Aeronautics –
     Australia – History. I. Title.

629.1300922

ISBN 0 7022 2365 4

To the memory of my friend Denys Dalton

"The engine is the heart of the aeroplane
but the pilot is its soul."

Sir Walter Raleigh, 1922

Contents

Illustrations

Vickers Vimy G-EAOU, hand-filled from petrol cans
In recognition of the 1919 England-Australia flight,
    Charleville produced a special montage depicting the
    crew, aircraft and the route
Photograph taken by Lt Hudson Fysh during the epic
    overland air route survey
Hudson Fysh and Arthur Baird with the Qantas BE 2 E
Jack Haslett and Ivy Coates. In November 1922, with pilot
    Paul McGinness and engineer Jack Haslett, Ivy Coates
    flew on the return leg of Qantas' first scheduled airline
    service − between Charleville and Cloncurry
Qantas − 1930
DH 60 Moths, DH 80 Puss Moth, DH 61 Giant Moth and a
    DH 50J outside the Qantas hangar at Brisbane's
    Archerfield Airport
Jack Treacy
The burial of Baron von Richthofen
An RE 8 No. 3 Squadron AFC
Treacy's tiny Avro Baby
The *Star of Townsville* with Captain Jack Treacy
Hubert Wilkins and his pilot Carl Ben Eielson at Point Bar-
    row prior to their trans-polar flight
Wilkins and Eielson flew a ski-equipped version of
    Lockheed's successful Vega monopolane
In 1931 Wilkins climbed down the hatch of an old US Navy
    submarine he named *Nautilus* and attempted to sail
    under the North Pole
Australia's quiet hero, Bert Hinkler
Hinkler with his beloved Avro Avian
Hinkler and his wife Nancy on the eastbound flight from
    Perth
The streets of Brisbane are jammed as Hinkler and his
    Avro Avian parade through the city
Jessie "Chubbie" Miller photographed in the USA
Chubbie Miller made headlines in 1927 when she became
    the first woman to fly from England to Australia as a pas-
    senger in Captain Bill Lancaster's Avro Avian *Red Rose*

Acknowledgments

It would have been impossible to have researched these stories without the assistance of many patient and helpful people.

Among those who contributed greatly, two very gracious women immediately come to mind: Vera Cotton who helped so much with the story of her brother and Lores Bonney for recalling details of her epic flights. That early meeting with Lores has established a life-long friendship.

For the clue that led me to long-forgotten air ace Captain Robert Little I am indebted to friend and fellow flyer Jerry O'Day. An ex-Royal Australian Navy pilot, he insisted that Australia's greatest air ace had been a naval airman. His enthusiasm was the catalyst of a two-year hunt for information. It was another former flying colleague, Wing Commander Michael Parer, who first brought the exploits of his famous uncle Ray Parer to my attention.

I met the late Jack Treacy when involved with the official government celebrations commemorating the fiftieth anniversary of the *Southern Cross* trans-Pacific flight. It was well past midnight during a drive back to his hotel that Jack's memories of Richthofen casually slipped out. The next day he generously made time to talk of his years as one of Australia's first commercial pilots.

For helping me to locate old clippings and photographs of Chubbie Miller's American flying days, and Harry Houdini's Australian exploits, I must thank Larry Wilson and the staff of the library of the National Air & Space

Museum in Washington, D.C. The staff in the library of Queensland Newspapers also provided me with a great deal of assistance.

Many other people have helped. Friends, colleagues, even complete strangers, assisted with an idea here or a snippet of information there. My thanks to them all. And especially to my walking thesaurus, spell-checker, copy editor, critic, friend and wife Susan.

Preface

Australia has produced more than its share of pioneer flyers: fearless men and women who helped establish aviation in the adventuring years when pilots flew in helmets,
goggles and open cockpits. They had none of the array of
flight instruments, automatic pilots and radio navigation
systems that cram today's hi-tech cockpits. Their wood,
wire and fabric aircraft had only a few crude instruments
and to fly them pilots relied on "eye-balling" the horizon.
If forced to fly at night, or if they were caught in cloud, survival often depended on a finely tuned "seat-of-the-pants"
skill — an uncanny ability that natural pilots have to sense
their aeroplane's flight attitude and detect the slightest
change.

In *By the Seats of Their Pants* I write about those wind-
in-the-wires days of open cockpits and leather helmets. Indeed I was fortunate that two adventuring flyers who
learned their trade in those heady days became my close
friends. One of them is Lores Bonney who only now, sixty
years after her first pioneering flight, is receiving long-
overdue recognition for her remarkable achievements.
The other was the late Denys Dalton.

Denys' aviation career began back in the 1930s. His
seat-of-the-pants flying started in Finland. As an RAF-
trained mercenary pilot he flew outdated Bristol Bulldog
biplanes for the beleaguered Finnish Air Force against the
might of Russia. During the Second World War he flew
Hurricanes and Spitfires.

When we first met, Denys and his wife Norma owned the Gold Coast's fabled *El Rancho* restaurant. He had given up professional flying and by then (almost always accompanied by Norma) flew for relaxation and the sheer love of it. I was an Examiner of Airmen with DCA — Australia's Department of Civil Aviation.

It was at Denys' invitation that I was able to experience first-hand the compulsion and challenge of setting an around-the-world speed record. Our record was achieved in a modern and sophisticated airplane. Nevertheless, because of it, I can better understand the thrills, frustration, despair and exhilaration that attended the efforts of those marvellous early record-breakers. I still wonder at how they managed in their oldtime, and often unreliable, machines and marvel at their courage.

Denys Dalton's story makes a fitting ending to *By the Seats of Their Pants*. Had he been born a decade earlier, I have no doubt that Denys would have been flying with "Smithy" in the *Southern Cross*, challenging America's Wiley Post to be first to circle the world, or trying to outspeed Howard Hughes' racer. For, above all, Denys loved flying and challenge.

In the dramatic 122 hours and forty minutes we spent cooped up in the cockpit of "Victor-Kilo-Echo", Denys and I learnt more about each other, and ourselves, than friends normally find out in a lifetime. I miss Denys, and dedicate this book to him.

Terry Gwynn-Jones
Brisbane 1991

1

"The First Flight in the Antipodes"

Mystery still clouds the identity of Australia's first aviator. Was it a forgotten Adelaide mechanic named Fred Custance or the legendary American magician and escapologist, Harry Houdini? Pinning down the truth is like trying to shackle the elusive Houdini.

In February 1910, when "The Great Houdini" arrived in Melbourne to star at the Tivoli Theatre, aviation was the latest fad. In the seven years since America's Wright brothers had opened the age of powered flight, France had leapt into the lead. In 1909 Henri Farman had flown non-stop for almost 250 kilometres and another Frenchman, Louis Blériot, had crossed the English Channel.

Although Blériot's flight spanned only 36 kilometres, it was the first time an aeroplane had flown over water between two great nations. It was to become known as one of the three great epochal flights marking the progress of aviation. Like Charles Lindbergh's Atlantic crossing eighteen years later, and Neil Armstrong's moon landing in 1969, Blériot's Channel crossing evoked unprecedented international attention, thereby opening new doors to aviation's future.

Besides firing the public imagination, Blériot had set governments worrying about the invincibility of their navies. While over-optimistic journalists proclaimed that the age of international air travel was at hand, others (more correctly) focused on the future military implications. In England, the safe, secure little island guarded by its Royal

Navy, London's *Daily Telegraph* editorialised: "No Englishman can learn of the voyage of Blériot without emoting that the day of Britain's impregnability has passed away," it lamented, prophesying: "Airpower will become as vital to us as sea power has ever been." Across the Channel, a French cartoonist depicted the ghost of Napoleon looking at Blériot's plane asking: "Why not a hundred years earlier?"

A month later, in August 1909, while Harry Houdini was touring Europe, half a million cheering spectators attended the world's first airshow, at Reims in France. Hearing about its unprecedented success as a crowd-pulling attraction, it is little wonder that Houdini began wondering about employing an aeroplane as an added attraction to one of his outdoor escape stunts.

Royalty, heads of state, military leaders and the cream of European society were at the week-long Reims airshow. They were attracted by the novel machines, flamboyant flyers and the specially built grandstands, restaurants and gardens. It became the social event of the year. Hotel suites fetched $500 ($50 000 today) for the week and the tiniest room in the humblest *pension* cost $70. Cafes ran out of food and halls were turned into dormitories.

On the first morning, more than 100 000 flocked to the specially cleared area on Bethany Plain. Not since Joan of Arc and her army camped there five centuries earlier had such a crowd gathered. Despite heavy rain, the crowd remained; in the late afternoon, they were rewarded by the sight of seven aircraft in the air at the same time. "It was a spectacle never before witnessed in the history of the world," a British journalist reported to his London office.

During the week, only twenty-three of the thirty-eight aircraft on display eventually got airborne. At one stage, the remains of twelve crashed machines littered the aerodrome, testifying to the unreliability of early planes and the inexperience of many pilots. Those flyers who did get airborne attracted incredible displays of hero worship, particularly the French airmen, whose antics made them the favourites with the partisan crowd.

Hubert Latham flew around the airfield in pouring rain, nonchalantly rolling and lighting cigarettes. Young Étienne Bunau-Varilla, who had just received his Voisin biplane as a graduation present, tipped his hat at the crowd each time he passed the grandstand. But none matched the audacity of Emile Ruchonnet, who had purchased his Antoinette monoplane only two days before Reims and made his first real flight – just over a mile – in front of the gathering. Such were the flying fools of aviation's age of innocence.

Within two months of Reims, the public flooded through the turnstiles at similar aviation meets held in England, Germany and Italy in the autumn of 1909. They were there for the excitement and the sheer spectacle, and to cheer their favourites. To the crowds, aviation was a life-and-death spectacle; an aerial entertainment which aroused emotions similar to those felt by the aficionados of the bullfights; man versus machine in an aerial arena. It would take years before they would even start to consider the aeroplane as a vehicle of transportation.

While performing in Germany, Harry Houdini purchased a French-built Voisin biplane. In those days there was no such thing as formal in-flight instruction, and learning to fly was a matter of personal trial and error. On 29 November 1909, in Hamburg, a cautious Houdini took out an insurance policy in case of injury – the first aviation policy ever written – and attempted to make his first flight. It ended when he wrecked the biplane before getting airborne. Undeterred, he gave orders for it to be repaired and crated in time to accompany him on his forthcoming Australian tour.

The great aviation exposition at Reims had publicly demonstrated just how far aviation had progressed in the six years since the Wright brothers first flight at Kitty Hawk. To those perceptive enough to look beyond the fail-

ure of the lesser lights and concentrate on the performance
of the leading flyers and their aircraft, it was clear that the
aeroplane had come of age as the world's new practical
vehicle. Attending Reims was David Lloyd George – soon
to become Prime Minister of Great Britain. He wrote:
"Flying machines are no longer dreams. They are an established fact. The possibilities of this new system are infi-
nite. I feel, as a Britisher, rather ashamed that we are so
completely out of it."

Australia, too, was "completely out of it". Even though
Sydney inventor Lawrence Hargrave had effectively
solved the aerodynamics of flight almost twenty years earlier, Australia was still waiting to record its first powered
flight. Hargrave's experiments with man-carrying box-
kites had placed the former astronomer at the leading edge
of aviation research. However, unable to build a suitable
engine to transform his kite into an aeroplane, Hargrave
saw the Wright brothers and European designers successfully adapt his theories. Indeed, in common with many European airplanes, the wings of Houdini's Voisin biplane
were based on the man-carrying box-kites designed and
flown by Hargrave in 1894.

The nation's only formal aviation organisation was the
Aerial League of Australia, a band of dedicated glider enthusiasts. Its treasurer and most active member was
Punch and *Bulletin* cartoonist George Augustine Taylor.
In 1909 Taylor had made Australia's first heavier-than-air
flight in a biplane glider. A subsequent plan to convert his
glider to powered flight was frustrated by the lack of a sufficiently light and powerful engine. Realising that a financial incentive was needed to promote the flagging cause of
Australian aviation, Taylor goaded the government into
offering a prize of £5000 (worth at least $100 000 today)
for the first successful Australian-built powered aeroplane. Unfortunately the competition set unrealistic re-
quirements. One was the absurd stipulation that the

aeroplane should be able to "poise" – a vague term which was then interpreted to mean hovering like a helicopter.

There was a faltering attempt at powered flight in Sydney's Victoria Park in December 1909. Thousands paid to attend an optimistically named "Flying Fortnight" sponsored by showmen J. and N. Tait. They were promised that an Englishman named Colin Defries would "soar into the heavens" aboard an imported Wright biplane named *Stella*. Bored with interminable delays, the frustrated crowd yelled "have a go" and Defries finally obliged. After scattering photographers during an unsuccessful take-off run, he crashed into a post on the next attempt.

A few days later, in front of a much smaller crowd, Defries bounced uncertainly into the air. Unfortunately, the rushing slipstream dislodged his wide-brimmed hat. Grabbing for it, Defries let go of the control lever and his aircraft plunged into the ground. "I should not have worn my everyday hat," the would-be birdman lamented after emerging from the wreckage.

The Great Houdini arrived in Australia early in 1910 aboard the P&O liner *S.S. Malwa*. It was hard to believe that the supremely confident showman was born (Erich Weiss) of impoverished Hungarian immigrant parents, and had started his career as a boy magician in a circus. Houdini now topped the bill at theatres throughout the world. The world's greatest magician and escape artist, Houdini was brash and egotistical. He believed himself superhuman and was always searching for a new death-defying challenge. Amongst his stage props stacked in the *Malwa*'s hold, the Voisin biplane represented just that.

Houdini saw his Australian tour as an ideal opportunity to teach himself to fly – far from the prying eyes of the American and European press. Determined not to have a repeat performance of his Hamburg fiasco, he brought along an experienced French aero-mechanic named Georges Brassac. Besides looking after the machine,

Brassac was also hired to give helpful advice – based on the dubious flying expertise he had gained servicing the aeroplanes of several French pilots.

What motivated Houdini to take up the potentially lethal sport is unclear. As a top-of-the-bill entertainer he certainly did not need the "appearance money" that was attracting hundreds to take up flying in Europe and America. It is more likely that he saw it as another challenge to his "superhuman" ability to escape from locked shackles in any situation. It seems almost certain that he planned eventually to include the aeroplane in one of his fabled "escape" stunts.

By late February, Houdini's Voisin was housed in a small canvas hangar in Plumpton's paddock, at Digger's Rest, about 30 kilometres from Melbourne. He was joined there by a second budding flyer, Ralph C. Banks, who arrived with the rebuilt Wright biplane – previously used by the luckless Defries. Its owner, L.A. Adamson, the headmaster of Melbourne's Wesley College, was determined that the honour of making the first Australian flight should not go to an American. He instructed his pilot to fly at the first available opportunity. Describing the scene, Houdini wrote home:

> It will surprise you to know that I stand a chance of being the first flier in this country. My machine is assembled and we have had the ground cleared of stones and other obstacles and believe that it is the greatest "trying-out place" in the world. We have at least five miles circular to move about in and only two trees in the whole spot. A young Englishman named R.C. Banks has been given the job of taming the Wright flier.

Clearly appalled by the Australian government's restrictive customs regulations, Houdini continued:

> The duty on aeroplanes into Australia is more than 35 per cent and I had to pay £500 [about $25 000 today] on my Voisin. I believe that all countries in the world ought to have a law allowing the first example of new inventions to enter the place free of duty. The people [government] here are not keen

on flying and, until some good flying is done, they will not go after it.

Every morning for a week the two rivals sat side by side patiently waiting for windless conditions. In those days a lighted match was the commonly used yardstick for acceptable flying conditions. If it blew out, pilots considered the wind too strong for safe flight. Consequently, most flights were made in the calm of dawn. On 1 March, the suspense became too much for Banks, and he decided to fly in gusty conditions. Shaking his head in disbelief, Houdini wisely elected to stay on the ground. He wrote:

> At about six in the morning he [Banks] went for a flight, rose to 15 feet, and had travelled about 300 yards, when his machine made a terrific dive and he came down and entirely smashed the machine. It was a miracle that he was not killed and managed to escape with only a badly blacked left eye and a torn lip.

Despite rumours that an Adelaide pilot was about to fly a Blériot monoplane, Houdini waited patiently until 18 March. At sunrise that morning, a soft breeze scarcely ruffled the leaves on the gum trees surrounding Plumpton's paddock as the Voisin was wheeled out of its tent. The big biplane weighed over 500 kilograms and was equipped with a 60-horsepower ENV engine. From the small crowd which had appeared each morning, Houdini found half a dozen volunteers willing to help with the take-off. Their task was to push on the lumbering aircraft to help it accelerate.

Houdini climbed into the crude cockpit perched between the wings, then called for his mechanic to swing the propeller. Pulling down his goggles in true early-aviator style, Houdini twisted his peaked cap back to front — no way was he going to lose his hat like the luckless Defries. A reporter for *Fly* magazine wrote: "The engine snorted and roared, creating a pandemonium of sound as the whirling propeller cleft the breeze."

Showman to the core, Houdini had shrewdly arranged

for a movie cameraman to record his flight. Poised over his tripod, the movie photographer wound his camera's hand crank as Houdini's band of helpers pushed the lumbering machine. Like the Keystone Cops they tumbled away as the propeller bit the air and the Voisin suddenly gathered speed.

"The machine careered along the ground for a distance of 50 yards. Suddenly she jerked to the left and made straight for the trunk of a tree. Her daring pilot placed both hands on the lever operating the elevator plane, and at the same time tugged at the steering wheel. The machine then rose like a bird and, just missing the tree, sailed fairly into the air," the reporter continued.

The historic first flight lasted about a minute and consisted of one low-level circuit of the field. Gaining in confidence, Houdini made a second circuit which lasted for about three minutes. Following a brief discussion, he took off again. In an article entitled "First real flight in the Antipodes," America's *Aero* magazine reported:

> Like a sweeping hawk the biplane swung around the paddock, and then Houdini, boldly tilting the upper plane (elevators), made a sensational flight over the tree tops. In all three circuits of the paddock were made, three miles being left behind in just over four minutes. As in previous flights the machine rode back to the earth in graceful undulations, and Houdini, gasping with excitement and legitimate emotion, clambered out of the pilot seat to be received with renewed congratulations and cheers by the spectators.

The exuberant American threw his arms aloft in a theatrical pose for the photographers and yelled: "I can fly. I can fly." When a noisy wagtail landed on the wing above Houdini's head, he joked: "He's telling me that I can't fly worth a cuss."

Among the crowd that surged forward to slap his back were three young Victorians — Harry Busteed, Harry Kauper and Harry Hawker. The trio had camped for a week on the Digger's Rest railway station so as not to miss the flight. Within a year of watching Houdini, the three young men sailed for England, where each made a name for himself in British aviation: Busteed as a pilot and naval aviation inventor; Kauper as an aeronautical engineer; and Hawker as the test pilot of Sir Thomas Sopwith's fabled fighters and the man for whom the world-renowned Hawker Aircraft Company (and Australia's Hawker Pacific) was named.

Over the next few days Houdini completed fourteen flights at Digger's Rest. The most successful was on 21 March when he was airborne for over seven minutes and flew more than 10 kilometres. The *Melbourne Argus* stated:

> Houdini set off on a cross country flight, leaving the safe landing ground, and sailing intrepidly over rocks, walls and fences. He made a sweeping detour over the housing tents and the waterhole lying to the east of the flying ground proper. On returning to a zone of comparative safety he commenced another circle above the flying ground. The plane wavered and tilted up slightly. "Ah! cabre, cabre!" cried Brassac, the French mechanic. The word signifies the action of a rearing horse and it indicates that the plane, like the horse, will almost inevitably come to grief. "He had better come down it is not good up there," said a late arrival from Paris.

It appears that the "rearing" – today it is called pitching – caused by turbulence was worrying Brassac. He rushed out across the field waving a red flag at Houdini, who obediently prepared to land. According to the *Melbourne Argus*, the self-taught airman had completely mastered the art of landing. The paper reported: "Houdini brought her to the ground in perfect style, never slewing or canting an inch, and it was impossible to tell when flying ended and rolling began."

In May 1910, following four flights at Sydney's Rosehill Racecourse, Houdini was awarded the Aerial League's trophy as Australia's first successful aviator. However, an article in the Adelaide *Register* suggested that the trophy may have been given to the wrong man. It seemed that Houdini had waited one day too long. According to the *Register*, Fred Custance had flown a Blériot monoplane at Bolivar, 20 kilometres from Adelaide, in the pre-dawn gloom of 17 March. Describing the flight, it reported: "A few twists of the propeller and the machine was under way at a good speed. It rose quickly and, with the fences of the paddock as a guide, the area was covered thrice in rapid succession – a distance of about three miles."

The *Register* also described a second flight which Custance commenced after daybreak. It lasted only a few seconds. After flying less than 200 metres, the novice pilot over-controlled and crashed into the ground. Despite being thrown violently from his seat, Custance escaped serious injury and later told a reporter: "Flying is not much different from running a plane on the ground except that you experience no bumps and have a sense of floating."

The news that Houdini had been officially credited with the first successful flight produced heated controversy. There were some who could not accept the idea of a big-name "Yank" being favoured over the local hero. However, few people outside South Australia took Custance's claim seriously. Unlike Houdini, who had made his flight in the glare of publicity, Custance's only witnesses were three neighbours. It turned out that the *Register*'s report was based on their (and the pilot's) recollections. George Taylor's Aerial League doubted the extent of the pre-dawn flight – particularly as the Blériot was noted for being extremely unstable and difficult to fly and Custance had no aviation experience.

There is no doubt that the South Australian got off the ground. However, whether he safely completed a flight and had his aircraft totally under control was another matter. Understandably, the experts of the day were not prepared to accept the judgment of three inexperienced – and possibly biased – locals who had never before seen an aeroplane fly.

In Europe and America, a rash of exaggerated and un-proven aviation claims had plagued the Fédération Aero-nautique Internationale — the official world body set up in 1909 to control aviation. Accordingly, the FAI had drawn up rules which included impartial observers and formal witnessing procedures for all officially recorded flights. It appears that Houdini's flights satisfied the criteria, whereas Custance's did not. It is quite possible that the South Australian missed the glory, and an undisputed place in history, by not having the stage presence of his American rival and ensuring that his flight was properly witnessed.

In July 1910, while the controversy still raged, a young Victorian named John Duigan was preparing to set the next aviation milestone — the first flight by an Australian-built aeroplane. The 27-year-old pastoralist had con-structed a home-built biplane on the family property, Spring Plains Station, near Mia Mia, 120 kilometres from Melbourne.

Fired by newspaper reports of the flights in America and Europe, Duigan had begun his aviation experiments in 1908. Even though he had earlier spent several years studying engineering in England, Duigan had never seen an aircraft and had to rely on books, picture postcards and sketchy magazine articles. During his student days at Brighton Grammar School, he had displayed an uncanny mechanical aptitude, constructing superb models of cars and railway engines from odds and ends around Spring Plains Station.

Duigan's first aircraft had been little more than a wing with a hole in the middle for his body. It was a complete failure. However, his second was more successful. It was copied from a postcard depicting the machine used by America's Wright brothers to make the world's first aero-plane flight in 1903. Not having an engine, Duigan con-structed it as a glider. Tethered to the ground by fencing wire and fanned by a stiff breeze, it lifted him into the air. He wrote:

> By manipulating the elevating plane the machine could be made to rise. I soon found this type of machine very sudden in its movements and the front would bob up and down far too rapidly to be comfortable. In a real strong blow it would lift two people.

In 1909, determined to become Australia's first aviator, Duigan began building a powered biplane, assisted by his younger brother Reginald. Virtually all their materials came from the property. The aircraft's framework was built of mountain ash and red pine, and all the metal fittings were fabricated from wool baling straps. For bracing wires they raided the family piano. Meticulously the brothers tested each component to destruction and, not trusting glue, nails or screws, they bolted every part of the aircraft together. With the airframe nearing completion, John asked Melbourne's Tillaroo Motors to build a special lightweight 20-horsepower engine. His final challenge was to construct an engine mounting and design a belt drive system to turn the propeller.

As the work progressed slowly at Mia Mia, the brothers learned with relief that Colin Defries had failed to complete his flight in Sydney. The Defries attempt, and news of several other planned flights, added a sense of urgency to the Duigan project. For a while it appeared that the aircraft would be ready to fly early in 1910 until preliminary trials forced Duigan to make several modifications.

While this was going on, Duigan's hopes of making Australia's first flight were dashed by Harry Houdini. Though bitterly disappointed, Duigan was still determined to be the first successful Australian airman and, moreover, to fly the first Australian-built aeroplane.

On 16 July 1910 the Duigan biplane took to the air from a paddock at Mia Mia. Before swinging its huge chain-driven propeller, Duigan joked: "The machine only has a 24 foot wingspan and it will be a toss-up whether the propeller revolves and the machine stands still, or the machine goes round and the propeller stays put."

The engine sputtered into life and Duigan scrambled on to his precarious perch on the lower wing. Like the Wright brothers in 1903, he faced the doubly difficult task of testing an untried machine and at the same time teaching himself to fly. Modestly describing the first tentative flights as "tiptoeing along the ground", Duigan said:

> The first few runs were rather exciting . . . but I soon got the hang of things. The machine seems very steady and answers well. So far we have done only short hops; however it is something to have got a hop out of it without breaking anything, especially as the ground is so rough.

To improve his airplane's peformance, Duigan made a series of modifications. First he produced a larger propeller and replaced the belt drive with a motorcycle chain. Next he redesigned the flight controls. Finally he increased his engine's power output by re-boring the cylinders, increasing the compression and converting it from air to water cooling. With the Tilley engine now producing 25 per cent more power, Duigan's kangaroo-like hops progressed to a flight exceeding 100 metres. On 7 October 1910 he flew 180 metres at a height of 12 feet, with his aircraft fully under control. Gaining in confidence, he began staging public exhibitions. The most famous was at Bendigo's racecourse where, cheered by 1000 paying spectators, he circled the 1.6 kilometre track at 110 kilometres per hour.

Although Prime Minister Andrew Fisher proclaimed Duigan's feat as "one of the greatest in Australia's history", the airman was unable to claim the government's prize. By the time he heard that the "hovering" requirement had been redefined to mean merely flying in a tight circle, the government had closed the competition without awarding the prize.

Sensing the government's disinterest in aviation, Duigan sailed for England to further his flying career, leaving his bush biplane to gather dust at Mia Mia. (It would remain there until shortly before his death in 1951, when it was presented to the Science Museum of Victoria.)

In England, Duigan paid a struggling aircraft builder named Alliot Verdon Roe to build him an aeroplane. Called the Avro Duigan, the neat little biplane incorporated many of the Australian's ideas. It was the forerunner of the aeroplane that established Avro as one of the world's great aircraft manufacturers – the legendary Avro 504 trainer. Thousands were built during the First World War and, following the Armistice, many were operated by the first airlines – including Qantas. Alliot Verdon Roe's company eventually became one of the world's great aircraft manufacturers, producing planes such as the fabled Second World War Lancaster and the Vulcan jet bomber.

During the First World War, Duigan flew with the Australian Flying Corps and was awarded the Military Cross following a dogfight with four Fokker Triplanes. In the Second World War he served in the RAAF and was given an appropriate assignment for Australia's pioneer aeroplane builder – administering quality control at the Commonwealth Aircraft Factory.

Harry Houdini's brief flirtation with flight ended in Australia. On returning to America he sold the Voisin and hung up his goggles. His decision to give up flying was not prompted by a lack of courage – as he proved in the 1920 Hollywood movie *The Grim Game* by hanging in mid-air from the wingtip of a Curtiss Jenny. It seems more likely that great escapologist merely lost interest when he found that there was no way, as a pilot, for him to incorporate the fractious machine in his act. The Great Houdini made only one public comment concerning the controversy surrounding himself and Custance. In a letter published by America's *Aircraft* magazine in August 1910 he wrote:

A Blériot monoplane in Adelaide was reputed to have flown the day before I made my flight, but on investigation it was proven untrue and the Aerial League trophy, which I have here with me in New York, was publicly and officially presented to me. So the glory of having been the first successful Australian aviator rightfully belongs to the writer. Up to May 9th, the date of my leaving there, I had been the only human being who had flown a heavier than air machine on the continent of Australia.

2
Australia's Greatest Air Ace

Eleven to one. The odds were impossible. There was no way the lone Allied Sopwith Triplane could escape the swarm of Albatros fighters. The Germans were virtually queuing up to let fly with their twin Spandau machine guns. What's more, the hapless airman was not only hopelessly outnumbered but he had taken on the airmen of Jagdstaffel 11 — Richthofen's infamous "Flying Circus".

It would be only a matter of minutes. Or so it seemed to the group of off-duty "Flying Circus" pilots who watched from their airfield below. Among them was the Red Baron himself. They openly admired the lone airman's audacity. They praised his courage. "What a pity he should die in such uneven combat . . .!"

But as the minutes ticked by it seemed that none of the German pilots was able to manoeuvre into a position on the Sopwith's tail from which to fire a lethal burst. Time after time as one (and often two) of the gaudily painted Albatroses closed astern and prepared to fire, the Triplane out-turned the hunters and itself moved into an attacking position. Not only was the pilot eluding them — he was fighting back!

Ten, fifteen, twenty minutes went by, and still no sign of a tell-tale puff of smoke from the Sopwith's Clerget engine, a flash of flame from the fuel tank, or any of the other signs announcing the "kill". The pilots flying the deadly new Albatros DVs were being given a humiliating lesson in the art of dogfighting.

For nearly thirty minutes the daring pilot out-turned, outclimbed and outdived his frustrated opponents. Time after time he flew right through circling groups of the enemy aircraft, forcing them to scatter and not allowing them to organise a set offensive pattern. His tactics were as brilliant as they were unconventional.

The watchers on the ground were awestruck – not only at the airman's skill but at the fantastic manoeuvrability of his olive-drab, three-winged fighter. The display of one-man one-machine superiority finally ended when the Sopwith pilot, low on fuel, decided it was time to head back over the trenches for home. He flew west, hotly pursued by the straggling formation of German fighters. As they crossed the trenches, he lured them over a battery of British anti-aircraft guns. The pilots of Jagdstaffel 11 finally gave up the chase.

Later that night over dinner, the subject of conversation was the bold Allied airman and his incredible machine. It was common knowledge that British squadrons had been re-equipped with the new Sopwith Triplane. A few of the Germans had already seen and occasionally dogfought with the strange aircraft. But until that afternoon no one had realised its true capabilities.

Their Commanding Officer, Baron Manfred von Richthofen, had already realised the significance of the three-winged design. The extra lift area and short span of the wings meant rapid climb, turn and roll, which were just what he needed in his ideal fighter. He would talk to designer Anthony Fokker as soon as possible.

But who was the airman who had outflown eleven of his best pilots? The aircraft he knew had come from the Royal Naval Air Service's No. 8 Squadron based near Ypres. The unknown pilot had the calculating skill and flair for the unexpected that marked a true fighter ace. The Baron would watch closely if they met in the air. This navy pilot could be a thorn in their sides.

And a thorn in the side of the German Flying Corps was

just what that pilot, Captain Robert Alexander Little, an Australian flying in the RNAS, was to become.

The brilliant Victorian fighter pilot was Australia's top scoring "Ace" of all time. His forty-seven confirmed victories also put him eighth among Allied pilots and number fourteen in the list of top-scoring aces from all the air forces of the Great War.

He was showered with medals for valour: DSO and bar (the equivalent of two DSOs), DSC and two bars, the Croix de Guerre . . . all in a space of only eight months! Yet he is hardly known in his native land and is one of the forgotten and unrecognised Australian heroes.

Little was born in Hawthorn, Victoria, on 19 July 1895. He was educated at Scotch College and gained quite a reputation as the class daredevil. One of his favourite stunts was walking along the top of a high and very narrow wall – one slip of a foot and he would have been seriously injured in the subsequent fall. Steel nerves, quick reflexes and total disdain for danger were already evident in his make-up – qualities that were to become a hallmark of his aerial combat a few years later. Doubtless a degree of luck helped him to survive his schoolboy larks unharmed.

When the First World War broke out in 1914 he was working as a commercial traveller in Melbourne. He had developed a keen interest in flying. Like thousands of Australians he had thrilled to the exploits of the nation's early flyers. Americans Harry Houdini and "Wizard" Stone had barnstormed their way around the country; Parramatta dentist William Hart had become the first Australian-born pilot to hold a licence; Victorian bushman John Duigan had built the nation's first successful aircraft on a sheep station near Mia Mia; and the newly formed Australian Flying Corps had just started flying from Melbourne's Point Cook air station.

Little decided he would go to war as a pilot.

Hundreds had the same idea and when Point Cook announced the commencement of its first military flying training course in August 1914, the authorities were swamped with applications. There were only four vacancies for pilot training in the school's Bristol Boxkite and BE2a trainers. They went to serving army officers.

Realising that it might take years before he could be trained in Australia, Little set out for England under his own steam in 1915. Once there he found that his best chance of being accepted as a military pilot was to gain a civilian licence first.

He enrolled as a student at the Royal Aero Club's flying school at Hendon, just outside London. It cost £100 but he soon had a basic pilot's licence. It worked like a charm. Less than three months later, in January 1916, he was commissioned as a Probationary Flight Sub-Lieutenant and was posted to the Royal Naval Air Service Flying School at Eastchurch where his basic civilian flying skills were polished and refined in the school's ungainly Maurice Farman Longhorn trainers.

These pusher aircraft (which resembled a flying cage more than an aeroplane) were used operationally in the early days of the war but had been relegated to the task of training – and often killing – novice pilots. Student and instructor sat in a short covered pod perched in the nose of the open-framework fuselage. There was only one set of controls, so the trainee was hard up against his mentor's back and had to reach over that person's shoulders to rest a hand on the control column. From this awkward position he was meant to watch and feel the instructor's movements. When he was thought to have learnt enough by simply watching and feeling, the petrified pupil was sent solo. If he survived he carried on. No wonder there were such horrific training losses.

The problem was compounded because "instructors" were pilots waiting to return to the front, or those considered unsuitable for combat. Things did not improve until 1917 when Robert Smith Barry introduced a proper system. With dual-controlled Avro 504s, and Gosport tubes to talk through, he became remembered as "the man who taught the world to fly".

By early May, Little was stationed in Dover at the Naval War Station Flight. Their job was to stand by to repel German bombers emerging from the North Sea to attack England; there was little action. Although occasional Zeppelins had been raiding London since September 1915, the first aircraft did not attack the capital until a year later.

Little, who had completed his training as an "average" pilot, had yet to display signs of the skill and daring that were to come. His early operations with the War Flight were hampered by continual airsickness and eye troubles. Time after time he climbed from the cockpit whitefaced and retching. It was thought to be caused by the effects of the sickly fumes from the castor oil used to lubricate the early rotary engines. Unlike modern engines, they spun around with the propeller sending back a steady stream of smoke and unburnt oil into the pilot's face. Keeping flying goggles and the windscreen clean was a non-stop job.

Little was also experiencing problems of a different kind. By the time he had joined the War Flight he was married and not yet 21 years old. Their Lordships in the Admiralty frowned on the thought of marriage for any officer below the age of 25. It was better still if they could wait until they were 30 and not at war. This attitude persisted until well after the Second World War and was reinforced by the military's refusal to pay marriage allowances to any married officer under the age of 25.

But there in Dover was the problem of a young Australian pilot scarcely out of his teens, not only married but with a young baby. Little's Commanding Officer obviously thought on similar lines to their Lordships in the Admiralty. Young officers, especially pilots, should not have the responsibilities of a wife and children – it had an adverse effect on their capacity to display courage. If officers had to worry about dependants back home they would not be prepared to give their lives without counting the cost!

There was talk of Little not being allowed to continue with a service career. The crisis passed when in June 1916 the young officer was posted to France to join a Dunkirk bomber squadron. It may well be that an act of heroism shortly before he left Dover helped to change his CO's attitudes towards the Australian's bravery. The event was reported in the London *Times* two years later:

> His entire lack of fear was well evidenced at Dover immediately before crossing to France. A Royal Flying Corps pilot flew into Dover Cliffs on a foggy day and crashed. Captain Little scaled down the cliffs and rescued the pilot.

Shades of the young Scotch College daredevil!

His squadron at Dunkirk was engaged in attacks against the German naval submarine bases at Zeebrugge and Bruges. They were flying single-seat Sopwith "1½-Strutters" – a modified fighter that had been very successfully adapted to bombing operations.

With the change of aircraft, his medical problems cleared up. He was quickly swept up in the exciting operational atmosphere that pervaded the station. There was no shortage of action – unlike the phoney war at Dover. The young Victorian was finally in combat and he thrived on it. His fearless determination on bombing flights was soon noticed and his superior officers considered him to be one of their leading operational pilots.

In the autumn of 1916, the German Flying Corps was reequipping with the latest shark-like Albatros DI and DII fighters. With two forward-firing machine guns they were creating havoc among the Royal Flying Corps' slower, single-gunned fighters.

The RFC was also suffering from its close association with the Army. The old-school generals controlled the new service and most did not understand its capability. Their Boer War thinking was twenty years out of date – air superiority meant nothing. To them the ultimate weapon was still the cavalry charge and suicidal mass infantry advances. Consequently, RFC aircraft were not gainfully em-

ployed as a weapon in their own right in the early years of
the war. They mostly had been used in support of ground
forces as aerial eyes of the Army, at low level over the
trenches in range of countless rifles and machine guns.
Losses were staggering.

Due to such stagnant command thinking, machines and
tactics were not keeping pace with the German Flying
Corps. The Navy, however, without the confining problem
of masses of men on the ground to support, and with com-
manders used to planning tactics around machines – al-
beit ships – and not men, made much better use of their
aircraft. Unfettered by the Army's incompetent "Colonel
Blimp" leadership in the RNAS squadrons had established
a fine reputation. The Admiralty had also ensured that
their squadrons were first to get the latest aircraft being
churned out by the nation's vast aircraft industry. Meanwhile, RFC units were still flying "death traps".

Aircraft design was progressing so rapidly, as each side
strived to gain aerial supremacy, that new and more advanced types were coming off the production lines
monthly. Many became obsolete within months of going
into service.

By November 1916 the Royal Flying Corps was taking a
battering and the Navy was asked to send fighter squadrons to strengthen the Western Front.

Special new squadrons were formed. Among them was
"Naval Eight" – hand-picked from pilots at the Dunkirk
base. The squadron was re-equipped with new Sopwith
Pups, which were the first really efficient British fighter
aircraft. One of the pilots chosen was Bob Little.

The Navy airmen were quick to appreciate the graceful
little Sopwith Pup fighter. It flew like a dream. Very similar in appearance to the 1½-Strutter, but much smaller, it
had quickly been nicknamed Pup when the prototype
rolled off the Sopwith line. "The Strutter's had a litter"
some wag had joked. The name stuck despite official dis-
pleasure.

Both aircraft had in fact evolved from Tom Sopwith's 1914 Schneider Trophy-winning Tabloid. They were the first of a family of war-winning fighters. All of them were refined and touched by the genius of Sopwith's great test pilot, Australian Harry Hawker.

The Navy, traditionally the senior service, was the first to be equipped with the tiny fighter. Powered by an 80-horsepower Le Rhone rotary engine, the biplane weighed a mere 360 kilograms. Gentle and docile to fly, yet lightning quick to respond to the slightest touch of the controls, many old and bold pilots still maintain it was the best flying aircraft ever built.

Another Australian pilot had joined the new squadron. Sidney Cotton, a Queenslander, had just returned from leave in England. He brought with him several of a new type of flying suit he had designed and had had manufactured. The suit was to write his name into aviation history. Later accepted by the military, it was named the "Sidcot" flying suit and was worn by pilots right up until the end of the Second World War.

Cotton, too, had been flying bombers and relished the new role. Like other Naval Eight pilots training at Coudekerque, he was frustrated by the attention the base was receiving from a lone German bomber. Every day, at dawn and dusk, a lumbering Rumpler Taube unloaded its harassing cargo on the aerodrome. A few bangs, a few holes – not much damage, but it was annoying and, to Cotton, a damned cheek.

He decided it had gone on long enough. He started his own daily patrol to try to intercept the arrogant intruder. For several days, the Taube avoided the waiting fighter. However, one morning Cotton was patrolling at 18 000 feet when he spotted the bomber a few thousand feet above.

He pulled the nose of his aircraft up in an attempt to climb. But the Pup was already close to the limit of its operating height. In the rarefied air, the tiny biplane flicked over into a dive. Cotton passed out. When he regained consciousness he was down to 3000 feet in a violent spin. He recovered and landed but was in agony. Blood poured from his nose and ears. In the mad dive he had cracked an eardrum. He was sent back to England to recover.

Though the attempted interception of the Rumpler had been a failure, Little and the other pilots learnt from it. Firstly they realised that at the altitude at which Cotton had attempted to fight, the Pup was at its operational limit. Secondly, that the aircraft could survive such a violent uncontrolled descent was a reassuring testament to the structural strength of Sopwith's machine.

The situation at the front was reaching crisis proportions when the hastily trained squadron was ordered into battle. Little was soon spending five or six exhausting hours a day in the air. Three offensive missions per day was quite the norm, including the dreaded dawn patrol — flying east over the lines with the Germans coming out of the glare of the rising sun.

He was assigned to B Flight, commanded by another Australian, Flight-Commander S.J. Goble. Goble, who eventually rose to the rank of Air-Commodore in the RAAF was to make history in 1924 by taking part in the first aerial circumnavigation of Australia.

After only ten days at the front, Little "broke his duck". Taking off from the squadron's Vert Galand Aerodrome on a scouting mission, he intercepted an Avitatik C1 two-seater reconnaissance aircraft over Beau-mont-Namel. With the Pup's superior manoeuvrability, he had little difficulty in shooting the slower aircraft down.

By the end of the year he had destroyed a further four two-seaters. Five aircraft in six weeks! It may not sound much, but it must be viewed in the light of those early days of aerial slaughter. A pilot's life expectancy was measured in terms of weeks — some estimates ranged from eleven to twenty-one days. Flung into combat ill-trained, and often ill-equipped, many died from their first taste of combat.

Those lucky few who survived a few weeks were "old hands". Often 20 year olds with less than fifty hours in the air found themselves elevated to the position of flight and even squadron commander as superior officers joined the lists of dead and missing. The average age of the First World War fighter pilot was 21!

Thus, after six weeks and five kills, Little had established a reputation as an aggressive and persistent combat pilot. And his unit, Naval Eight, was the talk of the Somme. At a time when the Royal Flying Corps was hitting an all-time low, their reinforcing naval colleagues were taking the battle to the German Flying Corps. In their first two months over the raging Western Front, the newly formed squadron had destroyed twenty enemy aircraft and damaged as many more.

The famous German "Boelcke" Jagdstaffeln (Hunting Squadron) was operating in the same area. The then up-and-coming young fighter ace Baron von Richthofen was flying one of their Albatros DIIs. He was known to the pilots of Naval Eight by his scarlet-coloured biplane.

On 4 January 1917, a friend of Little's, Flight Lieutenant A.S. Todd, spotted the Baron leading two other aircraft over Metz-en-Coutrure. Rashly he decided to attack. It would have been enough to take the German ace on by himself. But with his two wingmen to contend with at the same time it was hopeless.

Richthofen deliberately held back until Todd was busily engaged with the other two. He then winged in on the Pup's tail and shot it to pieces.

"We saw at once that the enemy airplane was superior to ours. I shot it down, but only because we were three against one," the Baron reported with surprising honesty. It was his sixteenth kill. Following that action, Richthofen was awarded his long-sought Blue Max (Germany's highest award) and achieved instant fame.

However, of his eventual eighty victims, the "Red Baron" shot down only one other of Tom Sopwith's amazing scouts. It has often been suggested that when possible he steered well clear of combat with Sopwith aircraft. The record suggests that such might be the case, for only twelve Sopwiths fell to his guns. Seven of them were in the last month of his life when there were so many in the air that he was unable to pick and choose and was more the hunted than the hunter.

Christmas 1916 came and passed with Naval Eight still in the thick of the fighting. The pilots had settled into the routine of life at the front. A blanket of snow lay over the battlefields, covering the carnage in no man's land and slowing the war on the ground.

Squadron operations were occasionally interrupted by bad weather, but once the snow stopped and the clouds lifted they were in the air seeking out the enemy.

It was freezing in their open cockpits. No amount of extra underwear, socks, gloves, coats and scarves could keep out the numbing cold. After each flight, Little and his comrades crowded around fires and pot-bellied stoves, painfully thawing out.

They cursed the bitter skies of France that made a nightmare of flying but none would have changed places with the troops who daily died in their thousands in the mud, snow and ice-filled trenches below them.

By March 1917 Little's tally had reached nine and he had been awarded his first Distinguished Service Cross. The squadron had been taken out of the front line. They were based at Dunkirk for a short rest and to re-equip with the latest fighter to roll off the factory floor at Sopwiths – the revolutionary three-winged Triplane.

It soon became obvious that the flying characteristics of the new aircraft were ideally suited to Little's personal air-combat tactics. Only considered an "average" pilot, his success was due to his superb marksmanship. He realised very early that in the hurly-burly of dogfighting a pilot usually had only one chance to get in a telling burst at the enemy. Many squandered that chance by firing from too

far away or without taking accurate aim. They simply
sprayed long bursts of machine gun bullets around hoping
one or two might hit the pilot or the vital fuel tank and engine. It rarely worked.

The great aces got in close and concentrated on putting
a destructive burst of fire into the cockpit and engine area.
They made that first burst count.

The Australian was an excellent marksman. One of his
off-duty hobbies was shooting rats. It helped keep his eye
in and quicken his reflexes. In the book *Naval Eight*, published in 1931, Squadron Leader R.J.O. Compston DSC,
DFC said:

> Little was not so much a leader as a brilliant lone hand. I feel
> safe in saying that there have been few shots better, either in
> the services or outside, than this man.
>
> I have seen him bring down a crow on the wing with a .22
> rifle and break bottles thrown into the air while they were still
> travelling upwards. What more deadly foe could be found
> than such a man, armed with two machine guns firing at a rate
> of two thousand rounds a minute?
>
> Once Little came within range of the enemy he did not give
> up until the enemy was shot down, his own engine failed, or
> he ran out of ammunition. He had, in human guise, the fight-
> ing tendencies of a bulldog: he never let go.
>
> Small in stature, keeneyed, with face set grimly, he seemed
> the epitome of deadliness. Sitting aloft with the eyes of a
> hawk he dealt death with unfailing precision. Seldom did he
> return to the aerodrome reporting an indecisive combat — for
> as long as petrol and ammunition held out Little held on until
> the enemy's machine either broke up or burst into flames.
>
> On one occasion this pilot dived with such persistence on
> his enemy that he forced the machine to land on our side of
> the lines.

The Tripehound, as pilots affectionately called it, was
not a really fast machine. But in dogfighting, speed was
not as important as being able to out-turn, out-climb and
out-roll one's adversary, and herein lay the new Sopwith's
strength. Also, the spacing of its narrow chord wings ob-

scured little of the sky, thus giving the pilot excellent all-round visibility. This was vitally important, for to survive a pilot had to have eyes everywhere – even in the back of his head. "Beware the Hun in the Sun" the experts warned. It was frequently the enemy diving out of the sun's glare above the tail, or creeping up behind and below, that killed the unwary. Many a novice never saw the aircraft whose cunning pilot fired the fatal bullet – those few grams of lead that sent him slumping dead over the controls, or exploded the fuel tank in a flash of blazing death.

Little's calculated approach to the use of his aircraft as a fighting machine was illustrated by a modification he had carried out to his own Triplane – N. 5493 – which carried the name *Blimp*. To gain the last fraction of speed and manoeuvrability, he had the seat moved as far forward as the cramped open cockpit would allow.

After only a couple of weeks out of the line, Naval Eight were called back into action. Despite the assistance of the new naval squadrons, the overall picture of Allied air-power on the Western Front was bleak indeed. The Royal Flying Corps was being decimated, especially those still flying outdated DH2 "pushers" and elephantine FE2s. It was almost murder to order pilots to fly such obsolete air-craft against the new Albatros and Halberstadt fighters.

German superiority reached a peak in "Bloody April" 1917. British casualties were 30 per cent. Squadrons re-ported losing an average of two pilots a day. Then the first of the new breed of aircraft, Pups, Triplanes, Camels and SE5s, started to trickle through to the RFC units besides the fortunate handful of Navy squadrons. But it was to take twelve months to fully reverse the situation.

Navy Eight and her sister squadron Navy Ten, both re-equipped with the new Sopwith, started the ball rolling. And Little's contribution was unequalled by any other RNAS pilot during that crucial year.

On 7 April he decided to take the battle to the Germans

over their home ground. That was the day Richthofen witnessed the incredible sight of a lone British fighter taking on eleven of his crack pilots. Though the Australian was unsuccessful in adding to his score, he left an unforgettable message with the arrogant airmen of the "Flying Circus". The days of German pilots having a turkey-shoot at the expense of the ill-equipped Allies were numbered. The hunters were to become the hunted. Little had thrown down the gauntlet on behalf of Naval Eight and the next day he shot down his tenth victim.

Over the next fifteen weeks, Little and *Blimp* accounted for fifteen more enemy aircraft. Always his tactics were the same: manoeuvre in close – sometimes so close that the two aircraft seemed more like two comrades practising close line-astern formation. It took nerves of steel to get right in there, especially if the German was a two-seater with the observer firing back at you over his tail.

Once in close, the young naval ace would stick there. This was when the Triplane's outstanding manoeuvrability really paid off. As his prey desperately turned, rolled, climbed and dived in an ineffective attempt to shake its grim pursuer, Little was able to match every defensive stratagem.

He waited patiently for the moment when his adversary made that one fatal error: maybe fractionally relaxed a turn, slowed his rate of roll, momentarily delayed a defensive climb or dive. Possibly the pilot stupidly levelled his wings for a second or two, maybe through lack of experience or just from sheer exhaustion – dogfighting was physically fatiguing especially for the pilot whose aircraft had the heavier controls. The Tripehound's were feather light!

Whatever the fatal error, Little had the ability to immediately seize on it and strike. It may have only lasted for a second or two. But it was long enough to get a clear, no-deflection shot from point-blank range. And, with his Vickers machine gun spewing out twenty .303 rounds per second in a tightly packed pattern, he invariably made the kill. No wonder his squadron comrades named the Australian "Rikki". His combat tactics were so akin to Rudyard Kipling's famous cobra-killing mongoose.

The Australian military aviation historian Wing Commander Keith Isaacs wrote of Little:

> Little preferred in-fighting and would fire only at point-blank range. Once he flew so close to an Albatros biplane that he collided with the enemy's tailplane, and had to land with a cracked undercarriage.
>
> An enemy aircraft to Little was something that should not be in the sky, and scouts and two-seaters of many makes — Halberstadts, DFWs, Aviatiks, LVGs, Fokkers and Albatros aircraft — all fell to his guns.
>
> In most cases the impact of his close-in firing caused wings, tails and even fuselages to break up in the air.

Typical of his fearless disregard for the odds was an action that took place late in April. He was leading a formation of four Naval Eight Triplanes when they came across twelve Albatroses attacking a pair of lumbering RE8 observation planes. The slow Harry Tates, as they were called by Allied airmen, would have been doomed but for the Navy.

The four Sopwiths tore into the fight. Though outnumbered three to one, they seemed to be everywhere. In minutes the action was over. The Albatros squadron fled the fight, leaving five of their number crashed on the battlefield below. Little accounted for two of them.

Decorations came thick and fast. In May 1917 he was awarded a bar to his DSC. On 1 July a second bar. The French, too, had noted his phenomenal record and chimed in with their gallantry award — the Croix de Guerre. In Naval Eight's operating sector, between Ypres and Arras, Little was "Cock of the Walk" — the leading fighter pilot.

His off-duty hobbies reflected a gentle and kindly man totally opposite to the methodical aerial killer. In the few, precious hours away from thoughts of war he studied botany. In the shell-scarred woods behind the front lines he would search for wildflowers. These he planted and nurtured in a garden he dug next to his quarters.

He considered himself to be a bit of an amateur hypnotist. Later in the war, when he became a flight commander, he is said to have used this strange talent on his pilots. He tried to hypnotise them into believing they had greater courage and determination than the enemy.

In common with most First World War pilots, Little did not think of air-to-air combat in terms of killing another human being. The fight was to destroy another machine. The enemy pilot was in some strange way an aerial brother-in-arms. At a personal level there were feelings of great respect between the "Knights of the Sky" of all the opposing forces. This was illustrated daily with a thousand stories of the gentlemanly treatment often given to downed pilots by their adversaries. Little featured in one such display of chivalry over his home aerodrome.

A German observation aircraft was seen 10 000 feet above the Naval Eight base. It had been circling for some time and was obviously taking photographs. As none of the squadron's aircraft were in the area, Little ran to his *Blimp* and was airborne within minutes.

The German crew were either too busy to notice the Sopwith climbing towards them or had decided they could look after themselves against only one attacker. Whatever the case, the German aircraft did not run for it. Little recounted the action in a combat report: "He [the German pilot] dived down, but I caught him and fired on him. I shot him through his tanks and through the pilot's coat without hitting him. He at once came down and landed."

The dogfight had lasted about twenty minutes as Little forced his opponent lower and lower. He had indeed holed the petrol tank and put a bullet through the pilot's leather flying coat. The German, whose name was Nuemuller, realising he had no chance, and with his fuel pouring from the holed tank, force-landed off a steep dive.

Determined to capture the German crew, Little landed nearby. But before his Triplane had rolled to a stop, the wheels hit a ditch and the aircraft nosed over. An embarrassing end to the action.

Somewhat crestfallen, the Australian crawled out of the cockpit and walked over to claim his prisoners. The German pilot Nuemuller saluted smartly then, looking at his relatively undamaged aircraft and Little's upside-down Sopwith, said in perfect English: "It looks as if I have brought you down, not you me, doesn't it?"

During the wild, twisting dogfight, Nuemuller's observer had got tangled in the snaking coils of ammunition belts feeding the machine gun he manned in the rear cockpit. The Australian and his prisoner went over to the two-seater and freed him.

Little recalled that both the German airmen were officers and wore the Iron Cross.

"One of the Huns (Nuemuller) said he knew he could never get back home when he saw me attack him, so he landed before he was killed. He told me that the war would be over this summer as England was starving and that therefore the Germans would win."

Once back at the aerodrome, the German officers were put under guard while the normal prisoner-of-war formalities were attended to. Later they were released into Little's custody and he invited them to the Officers' Mess for the evening. They were treated as honoured guests.

"When I took them to dinner in the mess they were surprised to see meat and potatoes and when the sugar came on the table they nearly fell over, they had almost forgotten what it was," Little recalled. "Obviously German propaganda among its own forces had worked well and even Flying Corps officers truly believed that the British were being starved into submission."

As the summer of 1917 drew to a close, troops on both sides were resigned to another winter in the mud and snow of Flanders. Little's victories had mounted steadily and by late July he had tallied forty-one confirmed kills, in just eight months.

On 11 August he was awarded the Distinguished Service Order. The citation referred to his gallantry and skill in combat and to the numerous aircraft he had destroyed and damaged in May and June of that year.

When the award was gazetted in the London *Times*, Little was back in England. As the Navy's leading ace at the time, and one of the few to have survived a year at the front, their Lordships in the Admiralty wisely decided that the exhausted pilot needed a rest from combat operations. Probably they also wanted him to pass on some of his expertise to the hundreds being trained back home, soon to go ill-prepared into battle. Maybe his advice might help a few survive the first crucial days of trial-and-error combat.

Two months later, a bar to his DSO was gazetted. It was awarded for a series of actions during his last month in France. The citation read:

> For exceptional gallantry and skill in air fighting. On 16 July 1917 he observed two Aviatiks flying low over the lines. He dived on the nearest one, firing a very long burst at very close range. The enemy machine dived straight away, and Flight Lieutenant Little followed him closely down to 500 feet, the enemy machine falling out of control.
>
> On 20 July 1917 he attacked a DFW. After a short fight the enemy machine was seen to dive vertically. Its tail crumpled up and it was completely wrecked.
>
> On 27 July he attacked a DFW Aviatik and brought it down completely out of control.
>
> On 27 July 1917, in company with another pilot, he attacked an Aviatik. After each had fired about twenty rounds, the enemy began to spin downwards. Flight Lieutenant Little got close to it and observed both occupants lying back in the cockpit as if dead. The machine fell behind enemy lines and was wrecked. Flight Lieutenant Little has shown remarkable courage and boldness in attacking enemy machines.

Little remained in England through the winter. In October he was attached to the Dover station and shared precious months with his wife and infant son who lived in the nearby town. Though naturally glad of the chance to spend time with his family, his spirit remained in France with his Naval Eight comrades. Secretly he yearned to get back into action.

As 1918 dawned, the Allied air forces had evened the balance of power and by the end of January were gaining supremacy in the skies over the Western Front.

Richthofen's "Jasta 11" were still a menace, hunting in their familiar huge pack of aircraft. The Red Baron was now leading the formation in a new aircraft – a scarlet Fokker DRI. At a quick glance you would have sworn it had come right off the Sopwith production line. Its three wings, radial engine and stubby fuselage were an obvious take-off from the aircraft he had seen flown by Little to such effect against Jasta 11 the previous year.

The Red Baron had in fact discussed the building of a similar aircraft with Fokker. It is rumoured that the brilliant designer resorted to subterfuge by having the wreckage of the first Sopwith Triplane shot down over the lines secretly delivered to his works. There it is whispered he examined the design in detail and merely refined it to suit his needs.

Whether or not this is true, there is no doubt they were remarkably similar. So much so that Richthofen recounted that his first action in the new aircraft was a piece of cake. Over Zonnebeke he sighted a lone RE8 on reconnaissance. He roared in for the kill, amazed to find that the two occupants made no effort to defend themselves. The luckless crew of the Harry Tate obviously thought they were being approached by one of their own Tripes – Richthofen's Fokker was the first in the sky – how were they to know?

When less than 75 metres from the RE8, Richthofen opened fire. A burst of twenty rounds ripped into the RFC aircraft. They never knew what hit them. It rolled on its back and crashed.

Two days later the German ace registered his sixty-first kill when his Fokker outmanoeuvred a Sopwith Pup.

By March 1918, Little could remain inactive no longer. He volunteered to return to the front. Because there had been a change in command in Navy Eight, he elected to join No.3 Naval Fighter Squadron.

Naval Three was commanded by Flight Lieutenant Raymond Collishaw, the Canadian ace who was eventually to become the Navy's all-time top-scoring pilot.

Collishaw had earlier been flight commander of "B" Flight — Naval Ten. It was known as "Black Flight" because all the pilots were Canadians manning black-nosed Triplanes. Collishaw and his men had shot down eighty-seven German aircraft during three months of late 1917. With sinister aircraft names like *Black Death*, *Black Maria*, *Black Roger* and the inevitable comedian in *Black Sheep*, the wild Canadians had almost "out-circussed" Richthofen's gaudy group. Stiff-upper-lip British "brass" did not approve of such "showing-off". The RFC were ordered to ensure that all aircraft were maintained in standard military olive drab with no embellishments!

One of Little's last instructions to his wife before joining his new squadron in France was that if he did not survive the war, his infant son was also to be educated at Scotch College.

He was posted to Naval Three as a Flight Commander. Germany had commenced the first and most successful of five major offensives launched in a desperate effort to bring a quick conclusion to the war. The first attack was launched against the British sector, with all available reserves of men and machines directed to a single thrust. The German Flying Corps massed 1680 aircraft in the attack in support of massive troop movements. For a short time they again dominated the skies and British losses were heavy.

Little's new squadron was equipped with the latest Sopwith Camel fighters. Lacking a little of the agility of his beloved Triplane, they were nevertheless much faster and packed a more lethal punch. The Australian found the twin-Vickers machine guns much to his liking. The Camel was to become the most successful fighter of the war. Sopwith's classic aircraft accounted for 1294 enemy aircraft during its sixteen months in service.

He soon established a reputation as a real "fire-eater" among his junior pilots. His commanding officer Collishaw – later to become an Air Vice-Marshal in the RAF – wrote of the reasons years after in Keith Isaacs' book, *Military Aircraft of Australia 1909-1918*:

> The pilots in other flights were glad not to be under Little's command. They thought he was far too inclined to seek and to take too many unnecessary risks. He believed that it was a waste of time to adopt the usual practice to gradually accustom a fledgling to war flying at the front.
>
> He believed that a man was born and endowed with, or without, courage. Whenever he received a new young pilot he took him over the lines to "blood" him. Little led the fledgling very low over the lines whereupon all hell broke loose. If the new pilot followed him properly Little then went on with his advanced training. If he failed the test Little would have nothing more to do with him.

Quite a method of sorting out the men from the boys! But in a way it ties in with Squadron Leader Compston's assessment that Little was the brilliant lone wolf rather than a leader. In some ways it seems that he was still the daredevil schoolboy who walked the high wall. To prove he was braver than his fellows? Or maybe just to reassure himself? Little and his pilots flew in a war where you were either brave or a coward. Automatic, unthinking courage was the order of the day. "Your Country Needs You" was the watchword at home and wives and mothers handed white feathers of cowardice to men in the streets, civilians, whom they thought of the age to be in uniform but who had not heeded the call. It was a time of involuntary cruelty and early death. Better their sons die bravely than live as cowards, or so many believed. Small wonder the Australian ace practised such harsh and unconventional training methods.

Little had returned to action determined to continue his reign and maintain his position as the leading naval pilot. He found it becoming increasingly difficult. With the German thrust on the ground, all available aircraft were taken off patrol duties and thrown into a ground-attack role. Day after day, Allied aircraft concentrated on strafing advancing troop concentrations.

Soon after his return to active duty, all British air units were combined into a newly formed service. As of 1 April 1918, Flight Commander Little, RNAS, became Captain Little of No. 203 Squadron Royal Air Force.

Three weeks later, on the same day that Richthofen fell to a bullet fired by an Australian soldier (almost certainly Sergeant Gunner Cedric Popkin), Little was shot down for the first time. He was up to his old tricks of fearlessly attacking large enemy formations. The RAF official report on the action reads more like the scenario for a Hollywood Errol Flynn epic than a military communique:

Captain R.A. Little, 203 Squadron, attacked the rear machine of a formation of twelve enemy aircraft and watched it fall to 1000 feet near "Vie-x-Berquin" completely out of control. [The attack had commenced at 15 000 feet.]

Captain Little was then attacked by six enemy aircraft and was driven down through the formation below; he put his machine into a spin and his controls were shot away causing his machine to dive to within 100 feet of the ground when it flattened out with a jerk, breaking the fuselage just under the pilot's seat. Captain Little undid the belt and was thrown clear when the machine struck the ground. The E.A. continued to fire at him, but he opened fire with his revolver at one enemy aircraft which came down to about thirty feet. The enemy aircraft was eventually driven off by our infantry with rifle and machine gun fire.

It seems from that report that the days of reckless bravery were numbered – as became the situation in the Second World War. It was not just a case of destroying machines.

Eventual air superiority depended also on drying up the flow of aircrew. A new plane could be manufactured within days; a new pilot took months to train and even then he was a raw beginner at aerial duelling.

The RAF report also highlights one of the most shameful facts to come out of the First World War in the air. Allied pilots were not equipped with parachutes, despite the fact that they were being successfully used for supply dropping, and by airmen manning the hundreds of observation balloons on the Western Front.

It was not until after the war that the matter was eventually disclosed. Callous, blundering military brass had decided that if they equipped pilots with parachutes they might jump from their aircraft rather than face a fight. Instant courage at any cost! Their incredible decision shows just how little the generals were in touch with the reality of modern warfare or understood the men under their command.

When survivors of the slaughter in the air learned the truth, disbelief of such a murderous decision turned to fury. Many wept, remembering watching comrades jump thousands of feet to their death rather than face a slow, agonising incineration in their burning aircraft. Those who flew the RE8s – a notorious burner – suffered most, including the Australian squadrons equipped with the ill-fated aircraft frequently attacked by Richthofen's new arrivals for combat training.

On 27 May 1918, Captain Little's combat score had reached forty-seven confirmed kills – only three off the magic half-century. He was leading the pack of ex-naval pilots, though closely followed by Collishaw.

Enemy aircraft were becoming hard to find as the Allies were again in control of the air. But a few weeks earlier the Germans had started a new tactic. Giant twin-engined Gotha GIV bombers were crossing the lines at night, bombing areas behind the British lines. Collishaw and Little had decided to try to bring one down.

Their Camels were not equipped for night flying. With no cockpit lights and no blind-flying instruments, the flights themselves were a very risky business. The pair had been airborne on several moonlit nights without sighting one of the huge aircraft.

On the night of 27 May, Gothas were reported bombing nearby St Omer. Collishaw was on leave in England and Bob Little had been placed in command of No. 203. It was full moon and as soon as the report came through the Australian ordered his Camel (No.B.6318) prepared for action.

Within minutes he was strapped in and warming up the snarling 230-horsepower Bentley engine. At 9 p.m. he waved the chocks away and squadron pilots watched as he took off across the field and disappeared in the night. They listened to the roar of the engine mute with distance — and then silence.

Back in the Officers' Mess, No. 203 pilots waited for his return. His groundcrew stood, ears tuned for the first sound of the lone Camel. It never returned. When his petrol endurance was known to have expired, Little was posted "Missing". Just a simple chalk entry against his name on the operations board. It seemed unbelievable. Little's pilots had begun to feel, like the Australian himself, that he was divinely protected. Maybe he had got lost and force-landed somewhere or, short of fuel, had decided to put down at another airfield.

Aircraft were not yet equipped with radio, so there was no way of knowing what might have happened to their commander.

Early next morning, a message from the Army reached No. 203's Ezil le Hamel base stating that Little had been shot down near the village of Norviz. He was dead.

The exact details of the gallant Australian's final combat are sketchy. It appears that he found his Gotha and was positioned for attack. Knowing his tactics, chances are that he closed to point-blank range, lining up on the blue exhaust flames of the bomber's twin Mercedes Benz engines. He would have had no trouble catching up, as the lumbering giant had a top speed of only 140 kph compared with the Camel's 190 kph.

Hunched forward, peering through his fixed sight, Little was suddenly blinded by the sweeping beam of a ground searchlight. It was one of those million-to-one chances that seemed so often to spell the end of the great aces.

Obviously presented with a clearly illuminated, close-in shot at the British biplane, the Gotha's rear gunner opened fire. He could hardly miss under those conditions. Bullets from his ring-mounted Parabellum machine gun ploughed through the fuselage below the open cockpit. They passed through the doped canvas and hit Little in the thighs, entering the groin. To receive such wounds he must have already commenced to turn away when the gunner's finger closed on the trigger.

Though severely wounded, somehow Little managed to get the aircraft down. He crashed in the darkness on landing and died soon afterwards.

He was buried in the cemetery in the little village of Norviz, not far from the grave of another great Allied ace, Major J.T. McCudden, VC.

It seems fitting to believe that Little's death was caused by some strange quirk of fate, in this case the random sweep of an Allied searchlight. There is little doubt that had his presence not been glaringly detected, and he momentarily blinded, the Australian would have added yet another to his long list of kills.

But death under strange circumstances was the fate of most of the top aces: Richthofen by a soldier's gun; Mannock — England's top scorer — incinerated after a stray bullet from the ground pierced his petrol tank; France's number two, Guynemer, just disappeared.

Though cold comfort to grieving loved ones, at least to their fellow pilots there was a feeling of satisfaction that these heroes – their nation's best – had fallen undefeated in their natural element . . . the whirling dogfight.

Thus Captain Robert Alexander Little, DSO and Bar, DSC and two Bars, Croix de Guerre, just 22 years old, became one of the 26 000 air casualties of the First World War.

His name should have gone down in history along with the man recognised as Australia's great ace, Captain A.H. Cobby of the Australian Flying Corps (Cobby ended the war with thirty-two confirmed kills), but somehow he was forgotten, as was another Australian who flew with the Royal Naval Air Service, Lieutenant Stanley Dallas, a cheery Queenslander who notched up thirty-nine official victories.

Possibly because they did not fly in an Australian Service, these two Navy pilots have never received real recognition. Maybe it was also because they did not return from the war to share the peace to which they contributed so much. Whatever the reasons, it is ironic that only a few dedicated historians recall these distinguished Australians.

Canada's top-scoring ace Billy Bishop served with a British unit. Yet he was honoured and is remembered today as his country's greatest ever ace.

No Australian pilot has ever bettered Little's performance. Nor will it happen in the future. For the days of the dogfight were numbered by the end of the Second World War. The eye of the marksman has since been replaced by automated missiles, fired from aircraft which may never even approach close enough to actually sight their prey. With computerisation and automation, combat supremacy in the future becomes more a case of technical advancement. Missiles, Anti-Missile Missiles, and so it goes; the mind boggles.

It is hard to believe that a few of those gallant men who flew with Little, Richthofen, Collishaw and others are still alive today. They must shake their heads in disbelief at the changes they have seen in one lifetime.

To them war in the air will always be the dawn patrol, the cloying fumes of castor oil, wind in the wires, rattling machine guns, and wheeling and diving over the Western Front: the Tripehounds, Fokkers, Camels, Harry Tates, and the men who flew them; the friends who never returned from that first patrol, and the few like Robert Little who commanded the skies for a brief moment in time.

One of those who lived to remember was Lieutenant Frederich Nuemuller − Little's unwilling prisoner. After the war he wrote to the Australian's young widow: "Because he was so amiable to me on the darkest day of my soldierly life, I will never forget him. He was in every respect a knightly adversary of the air."

3
Down in
Mid-Atlantic

The morning of 19 May 1919 dawned cold and grey in the mid-Atlantic. Homeward bound, the small tramp steamer *Mary* rolled and pitched in high seas whipped up by a strong nor'wester. On the tiny bridge the second mate and helmsman peered through rain-lashed windows. They had nearly completed the lonely watch. Steaming along the northern edge of the Atlantic sea lane, they had not sighted another ship for two days.

The only break to the bleak horizon was seemingly endless rows of intense rain squalls, looking like huge grey columns supporting the dark clouds above the leaden sea.

Suddenly, over the freighter's pitching bow, a low-flying aircraft appeared out of the rain and cloud. It circled the ship at mast height, its two crewmen waving furiously. The two sailors stared up in disbelief. In 1919 to see an aircraft was still something of a rarity — in mid-Atlantic it was unknown! America and Europe had yet to be linked by air.

The mate quickly alerted the captain and the crew, and in minutes the ship's rail was lined with incredulous sailors watching the circling aircraft. A succession of three red flares fired from the rear cockpit alerted the captain to the biplane's distress. He quickly ordered the lifeboat crew to their stations as the aircraft straightened out and descended towards the white-capped waves ahead of the bows. It skipped across a couple of wave tops and came to a stop, momentarily disappearing amid a sheet of spray.

Miraculously, it was still on an even keel and floating, although the 4-metre-high waves were washing over the upper wing. It was just as well, for it was two hours before the lifeboat could cross the 300 metres of angry sea to the half-submerged aircraft. In moments, willing hands pulled to safety the crew of the Sopwith *Atlantic* — Australian Harry Hawker and his navigator, Lieutenant-Commander Kenneth MacKenzie-Grieve, RN.

Soon after, the shivering airmen watched their aeroplane slip quietly from sight and with it their hopes of being first to fly the Atlantic.

Harry George Hawker, a blacksmith's son, was born in Moorabbin in Victoria in 1889. At the age of 12 he left school to work for a pioneer motor car firm. He was fascinated by mechanical things. Later he was promoted to chauffeur of one of the first Rolls-Royce cars in Australia, but already young Hawker had a new ambition.

In 1911, a British pilot, J.J. Hammond, was demonstrating the new Bristol Box-kite in Melbourne during an Australia-wide sales tour. Hawker and his two close friends, Harry Kauper and Harry Busteed, were in the crowd. In the frail contraption of spruce, silk and wire, the three young men saw the ultimate challenge.

Within months the "Three Harrys", as they were to become known, set off for England to break into the aviation business. Busteed joined the Bristol Aircraft Company, while his two friends were taken on by Tom Sopwith, whose fledgling company was destined to become the most famous manufacturer of aircraft during the First World War.

Hawker soon learnt to fly. Only seven weeks after his first solo effort, he set a new endurance record of eight hours and twenty minutes. This was no mean achievement, for his aircraft was a Sopwith-Wright biplane, almost identical to the crude machine in which the Wright Brothers first achieved powered flight.

A few weeks later, flying the same machine, Hawker

had his first crash. He sustained a slight back injury which, later in his career, would exact a terrible toll. Tom Sopwith noted in his new young pilot a quality rare among the daredevil aviators of the early days. Hawker was not only a born pilot, but also possessed an inquiring and inventive mind. He appointed the Australian as test pilot for the rapidly growing company. Harry Busteed was appointed to a similar position with the Bristol Aircraft Company and a keen but friendly rivalry grew between the two men.

Hawker developed a flair for design and contributed to the building of the Sopwith Tabloid, the forerunner of the famed Sopwith fighters. In 1914 at Monaco, the Tabloid won for Britain the world's speed record at the first Schneider Trophy Race.

He became absorbed in the problem of the most frequent killer of early aviators — the dreaded spin. At that time no pilot had succeeded in deliberately recovering his machine from the "death" manoeuvre. It was at the famous Brooklands Airport that Hawker made his first attempt to solve the uncontrollable corkscrew dive. A small group of pilots watched as he deliberately put his Tabloid into the spin. Apprehension turned to horror as they watched the machine whirl round and round in a near vertical descent. It didn't stop until it hit the trees in a nearby wood.

They rushed to the accident site but were unable to find the pilot among the shattered remains. Certain that Hawker must have been flung out of the spiralling aircraft and killed, they returned sadly to the airfield. Waiting for them at the Sopwith hangar stood their smiling friend. Miraculously he had walked away from the crash unscathed and hitched a ride to the aerodrome on the back of a motorbike!

Though he had reduced one aircraft to scrap, Hawker was sure he had the answer to the great mystery. All the rules of flying dictated that a pilot pulled back on the control stick to bring an aircraft out of any type of descent. He believed that one manoeuvre — to push forward on the stick and steepen the whirling dive — was the only way to regain control and break out of the spin. If one had the guts to try!

Four days later Hawker faced his moment of truth. Spinning down from 7500 feet he attempted his "impossible" theory. Onlookers watched as the uncontrollable rotation slowed then stopped and the little biplane eased out of the dive.

Thus the determined Victorian evolved the recovery technique that was to save the lives of countless pilots, a technique still taught today. But as was often the case in those early days, he received no official credit for his calculated act of courage.

With the Tabloid a proven design, Hawker convinced Tom Sopwith that he should take one of the aircraft back to Australia and demonstrate it to the Commonwealth government. The agile little biplane had already attracted military interest in England as a "scout".

On 9 February 1914 Hawker made his first public appearance in his home country. The then Governor-General, Sir John Madden, and his entourage joined 30 000 wildly elated Victorians who crammed Melbourne's Caulfield Racecourse and saw their home-town boy put on a dazzling display. The Daily Telegraph described the first of three flights he made that day:

> Hawker's machine rose with remarkable ease and gracefulness, and speared away into the teeth of the breeze with amazing speed. He shot up into the air to a great height, dropped sheer for a couple of hundred feet, turned his machine right over on its side, and then sent her nose downward again. It appeared at one stage as though she would dive right into the ground, but Hawker could do just what he liked with the aeroplane and when it seemed that he had got perilously close to the ground he shot skywards, shut off his power and came down with a wide sweeping circle. When forty feet from the ground he darted up and over the stand buildings. This was followed by an exhibition of corner turning. This evoked

roars of applause from the crowd which were repeated when Hawker landed.

Police had great difficulty in controlling the excited crowd. They had never seen flying like this; it was sheer magic. Before his second flight, hundreds had rushed around the aircraft. The landing which followed the second flight nearly brought disaster. The landing run was a railed-off part of the "home straight" and was barely long enough. The Tabloid ended its run just before the judges' box. Then Hawker's uncle nearly became Australia's first aviation victim in front of spectators. Rushing to help stop the aircraft from hitting the fence, he received a bloody nose when struck by the idling propeller.

On the third flight of the day, Hawker carried as his passenger Miss Ruby Dixon, daughter of O.T. Dixon, founder of the giant Kia-Ora food manufacturing company. She is believed to be Australia's first woman passenger. She caused quite a stir as she was helped on board. A journalist of the day wrote of her special outfit, topped with a "shiny black waterproof hat with a shiny black waratah stuck in the side". Young and good looking, she was annoyed by the lighthearted but embarrassing comments from the crowd. "You're on a good wicket there, mate!" a particularly vocal wit shouted to Hawker.

A band played *God Save the King* as they took off and disappeared over the horizon. To the crowd's disappointment, Hawker had decided not to risk another landing in the milling and virtually uncontrollable crowd. He landed instead on the golf course at Elsternwick . . . but not without incident. Ruby Dixon, in her day of "firsts", became the first woman involved in an Australian aircraft accident. The Tabloid hit a rough patch, shattering the propeller and wrecking the undercarriage. The pair were shaken but not hurt. The flight, lasting seven minutes, cost the young adventuress £20. Far from begrudging it, she was ecstatic afterwards. "I know what it's like to feel like a bird," she said, and immediately booked another flight with Hawker.

Despite a triumphant tour around Australia, Hawker was unable to interest short-sighted government officials in the Sopwith, which was a generation in advance of the five already outdated aircraft purchased by the Defence Department in 1913. None of them had yet taken to the air. Hawker and the Tabloid returned to England.

Throughout the First World War, Hawker tested countless aircraft for the Sopwith Company. He had been turned down by the Royal Flying Corps due to his back injury, now diagnosed to have developed into tuberculosis of the spine. He was already a very sick man whose days were numbered. Typically, he told no one. The most famous aircraft he helped Sopwith to produce was the deadly Sopwith Camel. A single-seat biplane, this agile fighter was feared by German pilots on the Western Front, and is well known by today's "Snoopy" addicts. The Camel, in company with the Albatros DVs of the Red Baron Richthofen's "Flying Circus", was one of the most successful fighters of the war.

It was not, however, until after the Armistice that the name Hawker was to hit the headlines. Early in 1919 it was announced that the United States was planning to tackle the Atlantic crossing with three military seaplanes. In England the *Daily Mail* offered a £10 000 prize for the first British aircraft to complete the flight. A dozen companies, eager to bring the honour to England (and of course further their own interests), took up the challenge.

Sopwith nominated Hawker to pilot their entry, accompanied by MacKenzie-Grieve, an expert Royal Naval navigator. Under the Australian's direction, a specially modified two-seater was built. Powered by a Rolls-Royce 350-horsepower Eagle engine, the *Atlantic*, as it was named, carried 1800 litres of fuel. It had a cruising speed of 168 kph at 10 000 feet.

A brainchild of Hawker was the specially designed undercarriage. To decrease drag and increase the aircraft's range, he devised a system whereby the whole undercarriage was dropped from the aircraft following take-off. He was confident they could make a safe belly landing on arrival in Europe. It is likely that the lack of a protruding undercarriage prevented the *Atlantic* nosing in beneath the water when it eventually ditched in mid-ocean and consequently saved the airmen's lives.

Twelve aircraft nominated to attempt the crossing were shipped to Newfoundland in April 1919. The flight was planned from west to east to take advantage of the prevailing winds. It had been decided to make the attempts in mid-summer when the nights were short and cloud at its minimum. The British crews were preparing at a leisurely pace; they did not plan to leave until June.

But the Americans put a spanner in the works. The word slipped out that they were planning to leave any day and route the flying boats via the Azores. Using this southern route they would benefit from the better weather in that area and have a good chance of beating the waiting British contingent.

Two British aircraft had already completed all their preparations and, on hearing the news, they decided to leave that afternoon. Conditions were still far from perfect. Weather reports spoke of heavy seas, low cloud and violent rain squalls in mid-ocean. But with luck the aircraft would be able to fly above the weather; anyway, the stakes were too high to risk waiting and being beaten at the post by the Yanks.

As Hawker and Grieve were preparing to leave they watched another British entry, the Martinsyde, commence its take-off. Almost halfway down the airstrip, this heavily laden biplane swung in the strong wind and crashed before getting airborne.

Hawker learnt from the other pilot's unfortunate mistake. He judged the crosswind perfectly. Soon after take-off, the crowd watched as the undercarriage was jettisoned into the sea. Loaded to the gills with fuel, the aircraft weighed over 2740 kilograms and the ascent was painfully slow. The *Atlantic* eventually disappeared into the low cloud.

Several hours later, at nightfall, Hawker finally throttled back to cruising power as they reached 10 000 feet. The sea was totally obscured by cloud and fog, giving navigator Grieve little chance to assess the drift. The Sopwith carried only crude navigational instruments and its "try-out" radio refused to work. However, just before the light failed, a small break in the overcast gave him a brief look at the breaking waves through his drift meter. He roughly calculated a new heading to compensate for the crosswind.

During the next few hours, visibility slowly worsened and Grieve even had trouble getting adequate star shots by which to navigate. After five hours they had covered 725 kilometres at an average speed of 145 kph. Huge cloud banks moved in all around and it became increasingly difficult to thread their way between them. The moon was not yet up and they still could not see the water. Soon they were forced to fly through heavy rain storms, huddled down in their open cockpits to escape the force of driving, bone-chilling rain. With accurate navigation impossible, the *Atlantic* was steadily driven off course.

Since take-off, Hawker's eyes had incessantly roved around his instrument panel. Engine revs . . . airspeed . . . oil pressure . . . altitude . . . water temperature . . . heading . . . ceaselessly surveying his gauges and keeping alert for the slightest sign of trouble.

Though great advances had been made in engine design and construction during the war years, such planes were still notoriously unreliable during extended flights. It was still quite normal for a pilot to land several times during a long trip to make minor repairs and adjustments. But on this flight the need for even the slightest adjustment would mean failure.

Emerging from a line of rain storms, both men had just

relaxed a little when Hawker first detected signs of trouble. The water temperature, normally a steady 80^0C, had slowly crept up to 85.6^0C. Not much of an increase, but to the experienced test pilot enough to cause concern. For the next two hours it failed to drop back and Hawker, with sinking heart, realised they had a serious overheating problem. If he could not lower the temperature, the water in the radiator would boil away before they reached land.

Sitting alone in his windswept cockpit, his brain numbed by the incessant engine roar, and surrounded by inky darkness, Hawker racked his brain for an answer to the problem. It was his years in aircraft testing and design that finally gave the answer. Between the radiator and water pump was a filter system. Some foreign matter, maybe loose solder, must have caused a partial blockage to the cooling flow. It was just possible that by switching off the engine and diving, thereby decreasing the water pressure in the filter, the offending refuse might float clear.

In total darkness, Hawker cut the engine and descended through the cloud towards the sea. The temperature dropped back, the problem apparently solved. A relieved Hawker restarted the engine and climbed back up to cruising altitude. An hour later the temperature rose again. They were by then 1600 kilometres out and past the point of no return! They made several power-off dives in an attempt to reclear the blockage, but to no avail. The cooling effect of the descent with the engine switched off was only temporary. Each time they attempted to climb, the water boiled. And each time they lost precious height.

It was now apparent that they might not keep in the air long enough to reach Ireland. They made a decision to head slightly south of their planned course and over-fly the shipping lanes . . . just in case!

Close to dawn the men faced another problem that was beyond their control. Ahead of them lay an unbroken line of towering storm clouds clearly visible in the moonlight. To enter their turbulent cells would be suicide. They had neither time nor fuel to attempt to find a way around. There was no alternative. Hawker opened the throttle and tried to climb over them. In minutes their water boiled. Steam belching from the radiator turned to ice in the sub-freezing night air. After three futile attempts, he cut the power and descended. Their only hope now was to find a way beneath them. At 6000 feet the moonlight weakened, then disappeared, as they entered a thick overcast at the base of the storm cells.

They were down to less than 1000 feet when Hawker finally picked out a shadowy horizon. He reopened the throttle but to their horror the motor failed to respond. In less than a minute they would be down in the water. Hawker worked desperately to restart the overcooled engine. The *Atlantic* was less than 100 feet above the sea, and they were preparing for the worst when the motor coughed back to life. They regained about 100 feet before overheating again forced them to level off and throttle back to a low power setting.

The Sopwith headed on towards the coming dawn and its inevitable watery grave, unable to climb, no height left to descend and cool the engine, the radiator now continually overheating. Their remaining water supply was steadily evaporating and they realised their attempt was over. At best they might stay airborne till dawn and sight a ship. But the odds against such a stroke of luck were so long that neither man cared to consider them.

With daylight, they had their first good look at the ocean and it did little to reassure them. The windswept surface was an inferno of white-crested waves. Their tiny dinghy would be useless in such conditions. They must find a ship or perish. And yet it seemed even the elements were conspiring against them. With daylight a series of heavy rain squalls developed. Within minutes the clear spaces between them became fewer and fewer, until forward visibility was almost gone.

Gale-force winds continually buffeted the aircraft and

Hawker developed severe airsickness. Both men had virtually given up hope when the miracle occurred. Through the fog and rain, about 300 feet to their left, loomed a small steamer. It was a wonder that they saw the ship at all, for it was at the extreme range of their visibility.

Hawker turned towards it and Grieve fired three distress flares. They circled the *Mary* at mast height. In such poor visibility it was imperative that they kept in sight; it was doubtful they could have found the ship again. As soon as Hawker saw the crew run out on the deck, he closed down the boiling Rolls-Royce Eagle, and made a perfect ditching in near-impossible conditions.

Safely board the *Mary*, the men were anxious to get a message off to England, but were informed by the captain that his ship carried no radio. The gale worsened and the ship's speed was reduced to two knots to combat the heavy seas. Captain Duhn recounted that an hour later he would not have been able to save the men.

Meanwhile, in England, the nation waited in vain for the arrival of the Sopwith. Once the plane was overdue, little hope was held for the two flyers. Ships in the Atlantic had reported no sightings of the aircraft and doubted anyone could survive a landing in the gale-swept sea. A ray of hope came with a false report of their landing in Ireland, then died when the rumour was officially denied. After a week the men were officially given up for dead.

Muriel Hawker had waited for seven agonising days in her flag-bedecked English home for news of her missing husband. She refused to give up hope.

On 25 May she received a telegram from King George V. It read: "The King, fearing the worst must now be realised regarding the fate of your husband, wishes to express his deep sympathy and that of the Queen in your sudden and tragic sorrow. His Majesty feels that the nation lost one of its most able and daring pilots to sacrifice his life for the fame and honour of British flying."

The following day, Sunday, she attended a special

church service where prayers were offered for the missing men. She had just returned home when the telephone rang. A reporter from the *Daily Mirror* broke the news that her husband was safe aboard the *Mary*. It had just signalled by flags to a lighthouse on the lonely Butt of Lewis off the north-west coast of Scotland.

Thousands jammed London's Kings Cross station for the airmen's arrival. It was as though they had succeeded in their attempt. Hawker and Grieve were carried shoulder high to Tom Sopwith's waiting Rolls. Wildly cheering Australian soldiers then lifted the car shoulder high. It was all too much for Hawker, who climbed over the crowd to a mounted policeman. He finally arrived at the Royal Aero Club on horseback!

In recognition of their gallant attempt, they were awarded half of the £10 000 prizemoney. A few days later King George invested the men with the Air Force Cross. It was the first time the famed decoration had been awarded to civilians. The King had earlier sent another telegram to Muriel Hawker. It read: "The King rejoices with you and the nation on the happy rescue of your gallant husband. He trusts that he may long be spared to you."

A few months later, Alcock and Brown broke through the hitherto impossible barrier when they successfully crossed the Atlantic in their Vickers Vimy bomber.

Hawker, now a national figure, formed the Hawker Engineering Company (later to become the famous Hawker Siddeley Group) with the support of Tom Sopwith. But in July 1921 he was killed while testing a new racing aircraft at Hendon. By then his injured spine was severely infected and he had been warned of eventual paralysis. For that reason he now always flew alone and, some said, with little concern for danger. For no apparent reason his aircraft was seen to dive into the ground at high speed. The explosion tossed his body 70 metres from the crash. Thus Hawker had finally succumbed to his paralysing condition in the air. The Coroner recorded that "he was not strong enough to fly and take risks like that".

The blacksmith's son from Moorabbin reigned supreme among the test pilots of the era of "Magnificent Men in Their Flying Machines". Of him, Thomas Sopwith wrote in recent years, "His was a great loss to the world, but it is some comfort to realise that the amazing progress of recent years: is largely due to the single purpose, devotion and energy of a few of the pioneers, among whom I would put Harry Hawker on the top line."

His name lived on in aviation long after the man and his triumphs were forgotten. It was the Hawker Hurricane fighters, flown by the "Few" of the Royal Air Force, that broke the back of the Luftwaffe during the Battle of Britain. For many years, Hawker's name was perpetuated by the giant Hawker Siddeley Group.

4

Aerial
Russian Roulette

Late in the afternoon of 2 August 1920 a battered biplane broke through dense bushfire smoke hanging over Darwin and touched down on the Fanny Bay Aerodrome. A small crowd watched the pathetic wreck of a machine turn to taxi towards them, then stop as its engine cut out. The fuel tank was bone dry!

Lieutenants Ray Parer and John McIntosh had finally reached Australia – 206 days after setting out from England amid the quiet laughter of their friends – to become the first airmen to complete the flight in a single-engined aircraft. The honour of first to Australia had fallen to Ross and Keith Smith just six months earlier in their Vimy bomber.

Although they set no record for speed on their journey, Parer and McIntosh indelibly wrote their names into aviation history. Theirs is a story of courage and determination against overwhelming odds that earned the ex-Royal Flying Corps pilot the lifelong nickname of "Battling Ray Parer".

Awaiting repatriation to Australia after the First World War, Parer heard of the £10 000 prizemoney offered for the first flight from England to Australia. A chance introduction to Peter Dawson, the whisky millionaire, produced just enough money to purchase a cheap war disposal De Havilland biplane. The DH9 was used as a day bomber by the RFC but had not been a highly successful military machine. Aviation was still trying to find its feet; aircraft and particularly their engines were still utterly unreliable. The De Havilland was no exception. Powered by a 230-horsepower Siddeley Puma engine, it had a top speed of 160 kph and a range of only 800 kilometres.

Close friends of the two men tried to dissuade them from the venture, which was little better than a game of aerial Russian roulette. But to the modest young Victorian, the pattern of life had always been one of accepting challenge, especially where flying was concerned. His friend McIntosh, though not a pilot, was imbued with the spirit of adventure and forceful determination of a true Scot. They made an ideal team.

Shortly before setting off, they heard the heartbreaking news that the Smith brothers had already reached Darwin and the race was over. Though bitterly disappointed, they decided to carry on. Even a letter from Army Headquarters concerned for their safety and forbidding the flight failed to deter them.

On the morning of 8 January 1920, a few well-wishers were at Hounslow Airport to watch the heavily laden aircraft slowly climb away and head for France. In gratitude to their benefactor, the letters "P.D." were emblazoned on the fuselage sides. Stowed on board was a single bottle of Dawson's whisky. "When you reach Melbourne give it to Prime Minister Hughes with my compliments," Dawson had said.

A storm over the French coast forced them to land in a rutted paddock. A tyre blew and the spoked wheel buckled. It took eight days before they got a replacement from Paris. Their progress across France was punctuated with frustrating delays. Water in the fuel system, a cracked exhaust pipe and a broken fuel pump caused unscheduled landings before they finally crossed into Italy. Between Pisa and Rome they were forced down twice. An oil leak and later an intense engine fire required hours of painstaking repairs. Finally they reached Rome with 30 shillings left and were again delayed awaiting funds from England.

On the next leg, to Naples, they narrowly escaped a terrible death. McIntosh asked Parer to fly close to the crater of Mt Vesuvius as he wished to photograph the active volcano. They descended over the crater and stared with awe into an inferno of bubbling lava and acrid smoke. Suddenly the aircraft dropped like a stone. Caught in a violent down-draught they plummeted out of control into the gaping mouth of the volcano. Desperately Parer opened the throttle and regained control. Fighting for height, *P.D.* cleared the rocky lip of the volcano with only feet to spare. They landed at Naples, two very shaken men.

Before reaching Athens six days later, they made three more emergency landings. The only day without problems was that of their arrival in Athens itself — Friday 13 February. A week later they had crossed the Mediterranean to Egypt, despite a rough-running engine and losing all their maps over the sea.

At Helwan Airfield near Cairo, a group of dismayed RAF mechanics examined Parer's dilapidated machine. To carry on across the desert would be suicidal. The fuselage was warped, the tail loose, the fabric rotting, the radiator too small for the tropics and the engine needed an overhaul. A swarm of helpful service ground crew descended on the De Havilland.

Five days later, *P.D.* was in top condition as they set off to cross the Syrian Desert. On board were a new set of maps and five handgrenades. The RAF commanding officer of Helwan had warned them that a forced landing in the desert could be fatal. "The Arabs don't like Europeans or aeroplanes. They'll cut your throat for sixpence." At their next refuelling stop, a well-meaning officer refused them permission to carry on. The desert had never been crossed by a single-engined aeroplane and they did not carry sufficient fuel to cover the 1000 kilometres to

Baghdad. "We'll wait for a tail wind," said Parer. The RAF men gave up arguing.

For six hours they flew over the terrifyingly desolate desert. The only sign of life they saw was a solitary horseman. Darkness fell and they had not yet sighted the River Euphrates. Fighting off drowsiness, Parer landed near a small lake and they snatched a few hours sleep beneath the wings. They awoke at dawn to find themselves being inspected by a small band of Arabs. It was obvious they were up to no good. Whilst Parer held their attention with a revolver, McIntosh quickly removed a hand grenade from the cockpit. He tossed the bomb behind a small sand dune. The explosion scattered the unwanted visitors and the airmen quickly started the engine. Taking off towards them, Parer could not resist thumbing his nose at the angry bandits as they ran forward brandishing their knives.

They reached Baghdad having crossed the Syrian Desert in eight hours. A baffled RAF officer said on their arrival, "It beats me. You should have been out of fuel 150 miles back."

Across the Persian Gulf to India they pushed on over some of the most savage country in the world. Twice they fought their way through violent sand storms. The resulting sand blasting was taking a terrible toll on both men and machine. Finally, on 14 March, they arrived in Calcutta. The engine was running so roughly that it shook the whole rapidly deteriorating airframe. They had 6 shillings between them.

For the next two weeks, Parer flew the un-airworthy De Havilland on advertising and stunt flights to raise enough money to continue the trip. They plugged everything from tyres to tea. With names painted all over her fabric, McIntosh remarked that the old bus looked like a flying general store.

On April Fools Day they headed for Burma. *P.D.* had been only partially overhauled with Calcutta's limited servicing resources. Two days later, with a fire in the carburettor, they force-landed on a small sandbank in the middle of the Irrawaddy River. In minutes they were surrounded by hundreds of hostile-looking natives but then, after firing off distress cartridges to scare them away, they were approached by a smiling chief offering help.

The fault repaired, scores of natives pulled the aircraft through shallow water to the river bank, where they cut a narrow strip out of the lush vegetation. Waving, grinning tribesmen lined their take-off run as Parer eased the aircraft over the jungle at the end of the crude airstrip and set course for Rangoon.

The next day, over the Gulf of Martaban, the engine began to misfire. Suddenly it burst into flames and stopped. Parer headed for the coast and warned McIntosh to prepare for a ditching. The fire blew out and Parer coaxed the engine back to life. It would only tick over roughly, but it was enough to stretch their glide to the small racecourse at the town of Moulmein. The waiting crowd dotted all over the field heard the engine cough and die for the last time. They had left insufficient room for Parer to complete his landing run and he was faced with a sickening decision. As soon as the wheels touched down, he deliberately forced the nose on to the ground. The De Havilland came to rest short of the crowd, a twisted crumpled wreck. Miraculously, however, neither man was injured. Parer finally lost his self-control. He hit out savagely at the milling mass of Burmese, until local police finally forced them away from the wreck.

Here they nearly gave up. The task of repairing *P.D.* seemed impossible. But the arrival of a local handyman and two Italian mechanics brought them new hope.

Seven weeks later the aircraft was ready to fly again. It sported a completely home-made undercarriage, a sawn-down propeller off an Italian aircraft and two Overland Motor Car Co. radiators hung under the engine to replace the one destroyed in the crash. Broken wood and rotting fabric had been roughly patched. Would it fly?

On 26 May the incredible looking contraption staggered back into the air. It would not climb above 1000 feet, but it flew! Seven hours later, with no oil pressure, Parer force-landed amidst irate players on the Penang Polo Grounds. Out of oil, the engine seized and stopped. Another complete engine rebuild was needed. A week passed before they left Penang. They arrived over Singapore when their engine seized up again. This time their landing scattered golfers on the Singapore Golf Club's seventh fairway.

Another engine overhaul! But this one produced an added bonus – someone unearthed a De Havilland propeller. Then, on their first attempt to leave Singapore, they ran into a "Sumatra", the local name given to sudden storms of vicious intensity. The wind gusts and cascading rain lifted half the canvas off their upper wing. After two terrifying hours battling the storm, Parer finally saw the ground again and returned to Singapore for more repairs. It took another eight days and two more emergency landings before they reached Timor. The more serious mishap resulted in another broken propeller and a wrecked undercarriage at Surabaja.

Despite a sudden bout of malaria in Timor, Parer was in high spirits. Darwin was only one day's flying away. At dawn on 2 August, they commenced the take-off on the last leg home. Halfway across the field the engine cut. The fuel line was blocked with perishing rubber. Poor old *P.D.* just could not keep up with the demands made on her.

No one would have blamed the flyers if they had given up at that point. Eight hundred kilometres of shark-infested sea to cross, away from the shipping lanes, in an utterly unreliable aircraft. Was it worth it?

An hour later they were airborne and, despite the airspeed indicator failing on take-off, they headed out across the deserted Timor Sea. Both men knew that with only a small change in the wind they would run out of fuel short of the Australian coast.

The wind held and they arrived home to a hero's welcome. From Darwin to Melbourne, huge crowds turned out wherever they landed. Thousands packed Sydney's Mascot Aerodrome; the utterly overwhelmed flyers lost buttons, shoelaces — even a coat tail — to the eager, grabbing hands of souvenir hunters.

Their glorious homecoming across Australia did nothing, however, to cure the old aircraft's bad habits. A broken wing spar was repaired at Brunette Downs; the engine failed yet again over Newcastle; and rotting wing fabric was replaced with folded grocer's wrapping paper on a beach near Tweed Heads. On their final leg to Melbourne, they were crossing Albury when the engine failed. Parer coaxed *P.D.* down in a cultivated paddock, but here their luck finally ran out. The wheels dug into a soft spot and the aircraft nosed over onto its back, damaged beyond immediate repair.

On 31 August 1920, special trains carried thousands to Melbourne's Flemington Racecourse for the official welcome home ceremonies. Parer and McIntosh landed in a borrowed De Havilland to receive an unforgettable display of public adulation. Prime Minister "Billy" Hughes presented them with £500 each and then led the crowd in a tumultuous three cheers for "These rattling good young Australians who have reflected new lustre upon their country".

The speeches over, the airmen walked slowly over to their battered *P.D.*, which had been brought to Flemington by rail. They reflected sadly on how they wished the tired old aircraft could have completed the last few hundred kilometres with them. For, though her unreliable and unpredictable habits had continually frustrated and often nearly killed them, they had grown very attached to "the old bus".

Parer reached inside, and from its protected storage place brought out the bottle of Dawson's Whisky for the Prime Minister.

The 22 400 kilometres from Hounslow had taken 237

days, but very little of this was actual flying time. The rest was frustration, repairs and delays.

McIntosh was killed in a flying accident one year to the day after their crash at Moulmein. Parer went on to pioneer commercial aviation in New Guinea until the outbreak of the Second World War. In 1934 he took part in the Melbourne Centenary Air Race from England to Australia. In a near repeat of his 1920 flight he again had to overcome an endless series of mechanical failures to his RAF surplus Fairy Fox bomber in order to complete the flight in four months.

Parer spent the latter years of his life in Queensland, managing two farms near Gympie until his death in 1967. His beloved *P.D.* is to be restored and put on display in a suitable memorial building.

Author John Goodwin, in his book on Parer, summed up this little-known pioneer in words that make a fine epilogue to his life:

> In Australian folk-lore a battler is one who constantly and cheerfully pits himself against odds and misfortunes, sometimes winning, sometimes losing and sometimes almost submerged in a sea of troubles and then fighting free again to have another go. If he learns anything from his experiences it is that he can find the sheer basic guts to overcome any obstacles — and that battling is part of the salt and savour of life. Australians admire a battler. That's why they gave him the name which stuck for the rest of his life: Battling Ray Parer.

5
Home to
Australia

It all began when Australian Prime Minister Billy Hughes offered a prize of $10 000 for the first flight from England to Australia. The "Little Digger", as the brash Welsh-born politician was nicknamed, was in England for discussions following the Armistice of 1918. In an effort to promote aviation and draw attention to Australia, Hughes and his government decided to organise the world's first long-distance air race.

The prizemoney was a huge sum in those days, equivalent to the annual incomes of sixty-five skilled workers! But they laid down some stringent conditions. The crews must be Australian, the aircraft manufactured in the British Empire, and the flight completed within thirty days.

London's Australia House was besieged by Flying Corps airmen. Awaiting repatriation in England, they could think of no better way than to fly home and win a fortune into the bargain.

Hughes, fearing that many poorly qualified and ill-equipped young men might recklessly risk their lives, asked the Royal Aero Club of Great Britain to vet all the entrants. Particular attention was paid to navigational knowledge.

By late 1919, six crews had been approved. Amongst those knocked back were a furious Charles Kingsford Smith — for lack of navigational experience — and Bert Hinkler — by a series of mysterious official delays. Hinkler, the great lone flyer, was later to suggest that the delays were to favour certain competitors. He wrote home, "Take it from me Hughes, with his big wide, Welsh, noisy mouth is feeding you the choicest sort of claptrap. He has already got more than his share of advertisement out of the belated flight."

First away was Captain G. Matthews, Australian Flying Corps, with his mechanic, Sergeant T.D. Kay. They left England on 21 October 1919 in the single-engined Sopwith Wallaby. Following a series of long delays in Europe, the two struggled as far as Bali, where they eventually wrecked their biplane in a crash landing in a banana plantation.

While Matthews had been delayed in Europe, five other aircraft readied for the 22 500-kilometre flight to Australia. But within days only one serious competitor remained in the air, the giant Vickers Vimy bomber flown by brothers Ross and Keith Macpherson Smith from Adelaide, South Australia.

Of the others, Lieutenants R. Douglas and J. Ross had died when their overloaded Alliance biplane plummeted into an orchard minutes after take-off. Captain C.E. Howell and his mechanic G.H. Fraser crashed in a storm off the Mediterranean island of Corfu. Lieutenant Val Rendle and his crew had made a forced landing in Crete in their Blackburn Kangaroo bomber and were out of the race with a seized engine. And the "tail-enders", Lieutenants Ray Parer and John McIntosh had not yet taken off in their battered old war-surplus DH9.

The Vickers Vimy bomber had left England on 12 November as the firm favourite among the strange assortment of aircraft. Designed for long-range bombing missions over Germany, it had a cruising range of 3850 kilometres. Two 360-horsepower Rolls-Royce Eagle engines gave the giant biplane a maximum speed of 165 kph.

Pilot Ross Smith was familiar with the route, except for the stretch over Europe. The highly decorated, crack pilot of No. 1 Squadron AFC, with two Military Crosses, three

Distinguished Flying Crosses and an Air Force Cross, had also been aerial chauffeur to Lawrence of Arabia on many clandestine desert flights.

His elder brother Keith was also an experienced AFC pilot and their two mechanics, Sergeants J.M. Bennett and W.H. Shiers, had served as Ross Smith's wartime mechanics in Palestine. They made a well trained and closely knit team, and were superbly fit following a special course of intensive training.

The four men were accommodated in two open cockpits, the two pilots in the nose and the mechanics in a specially constructed position behind them. To reduce weight to the bare minimum, the airmen had only the clothes they wore, a razor and a toothbrush each. In case of a forced landing they carried emergency rations consisting of tinned meat, biscuits and chocolate. Just in case, they added a fishing line and a few hooks! The remainder of the Vimy's payload was accounted for by a huge array of spare parts. With virtually no established airfields between Cairo and Australia, the failure of even the smallest aircraft part could ground them for months.

The first day's flight to Lyons in central France was a nightmare. Winter had hit Europe and blinding snow and sleet drove into the open cockpits. To the numbed airmen it was like a polar blizzard as the aircraft's forward speed whipped the precipitation into their unprotected faces at 150 kph. The windshield iced over, their goggles became clotted with snow and their faces were covered in icy masks.

The pilots took turns peering ahead, looking for a break in the weather. Each could only manage a few minutes with their faces bared to the fury of the weather, then ducked low in the cockpit to thaw while the other took his place. Even their sandwiches froze solid. In his log Ross wrote, "This sort of flying is rotten. The cold is hell. I am a silly ass for ever embarking on the flight."

Eventually they broke out of the storm 60 kilometres

from their destination, after spiralling down through a small break in the clouds. Their morale rose again following a warming rest. In Lyons they heard news of the progress of a French airman, Étienne Poulet, who had set off for Australia a month ahead of them.

Though not officially a race contestant, Poulet had decided to bring to France the honour of making the first flight to Australia. He was flying a tiny Caudron biplane and at this stage was reported to be past Egypt speeding towards India. The news was a stimulus to the Australians to carry on as quickly as possible. More than just the money was now at stake. It became a matter of national honour.

They raced on towards their next refuelling point at Rome, but strong headwinds forced them to land early and spend the night at Pisa. The following morning they found that overnight rains had completely covered the airfield in water. They had no option but to wait for it to drain. Conditions were little better the next day, and the rain had returned. Ross Smith decided to attempt a take-off, but the moment he started to taxi the Vimy became bogged in knee-deep mud.

In desperation he revved the engines to full power, but quickly cut the power as he felt the machine starting to nose over. Mechanic Bennett jumped down and threw his whole weight on the tailplane as the pilot repeated the procedure. Slowly at first, at a snail's pace, then gathering momentum, the Vimy moved forward along the boggy airstrip. As it reached a slightly dryer area it suddenly gathered speed and the mechanic made a mad running dash for his cockpit. Shiers reached down and hauled his companion on board as the bomber accelerated across the field and took off. A second or two longer and he would have been left behind.

Following stops at Rome, Taranto and Crete, the exultant Australians made a seven and a half hour crossing of the Mediterranean and landed in Cairo on the sixth day of their flight. The first of the four stages Ross Smith had plotted was over, and they were ahead of schedule.

At the Royal Air Force's Heliopolis Airfield, skilled mechanics gave the Vickers a thorough checkover in preparation for the heat and sand of the Middle East stage of the flight.

One of the engines had been overheating on the run to Cairo and Shiers quickly located the problem — a cracked induction pipe. The airmen and their hosts unsuccessfully searched the other airfields in Cairo and Alexandria for a replacement. A telegram to Vickers in London brought the reply that it would take two weeks to ship by sea.

A desperate situation called for desperate measures and it was the inventive Shiers who had the answer. Fetching the Vimy's supply of chewing gum, he asked his bemused companions to start chewing. When a large ball of the putty-like material had been gathered, he spread it around the fractured pipe, covered it with a bandage of friction tape and then sealed the bulging mass with coats of shellac. "She'll be allright now," he told his captain. Ross Smith looked dubiously at the makeshift repair, then at his smilingly confident mechanic. "We'll take her up for an airtest," he grinned. The repair held and the temperature of the offending Eagle motor returned to normal.

The next morning they left for Damascus, where they refuelled for the desert crossing to Baghdad. As they droned over the desert, it became obvious that they would not make their destinatioin by nightfall and they were forced to make an unscheduled stop at Ramadi.

The 10th Indian Lancers, based in the little desert town, gave the airmen a warm welcome. The exhausted Australians had hoped for a good night's sleep, but the wind that had frustrated them all day rose to gale force. At the airfield, the Vimy, straining against its tie-down ropes, was in danger of breaking free. With the help of fifty soldiers they spent the night fighting to prevent the aircraft from being blown over and wrecked.

At dawn, the wind dropped as suddenly as it had arrived, and in dead calm they topped up the fuel tanks and took off. They bypassed Baghdad, landing instead at Basra. From there, they crossed 1100 kilometres to Bandar Abbas.

The following day they flew the 1250-kilometre "hell-stretch" to Karachi, the leg that every airman feared most. It was over one of the world's most savage landscapes, hour after hour of jagged mountains interspersed with patches of white-hot desert. A forced landing on that sector meant certain death. Alone with his thoughts, each man scanned the horizon, silently praying that the two roaring Rolls-Royce Eagles would maintain power for the next few hours. Four, three, two, one hour to go! Seven hours and ten minutes out of Bandar Abbas they landed safely at Karachi.

There they were greeted with the news that Poulet was in Delhi. They had cut his lead from 3200 kilometres to less than a day's flying since leaving Cairo. Bad luck had dogged the daring Frenchman, who had made four forced landings. He had been delayed when his mechanic had been bedridden with fever. His aircraft had been damaged when overturned in a tropical storm.

They reached Delhi thirteen days out from England, and learned that the Frenchman had left that morning for Allahabad. After a night's rest they took up the chase. At Allahabad they were only a couple of hours behind Poulet . . . they were closing fast. At Calcutta the desperate Frenchman had made a quick turn-around and left just an hour or so before they landed.

The Smiths decided to press on immediately for Akyab (now called Sittwe). As they approached the little Burmese town late that day, the Australians craned over the side for their first glimpse of the airfield. Keith Smith was the first to spot it, and at one edge stood Poulet's tiny white Caudron. They had caught up.

The two crews greeted each other warmly and recounted their experiences on the flight so far. The Australians shook their heads in disbelief at the frail little biplane. Their Vimy towered above it. They were deeply impressed by the courage of the two Frenchmen for undertaking the flight in such a tiny aircraft.

Next morning Poulet took off an hour before the Vickers in a last valiant attempt to stay ahead. But the vastly superior performance of the Vimy put it an hour ahead of the Caudron by the time both aircraft landed safely at Rangoon.

The next leg over the mountains and jungle to Bangkok meant a certain crash if either aircraft was forced down. So, in the interests of survival, the two crews agreed to continue the flight together. Though the Vimy would have to fly at a reduced speed, it was worth the advantage of having the other aircraft available to go for help should the Australians come down. The same held true for the Frenchmen.

The next morning the Vimy took off first and circled while Poulet prepared to leave. The Caudron never left the ground. For twenty minutes the Australians circled before finally setting heading for Moulmein. It was obvious that Poulet was not coming. They later learned that the Frenchman was unable to get normal power from his engine, and subsequently discovered that a piston had cracked. His race was over.

The flight to Moulmein, then Bangkok and on to Singapore was a nerve-racking experience. At times Ross Smith was forced to climb the aircraft up to 11 000 feet — its maximum ceiling — to avoid cloud-covered mountain peaks. Flying in cloud without "blind flying" instruments, he had to rely on his airspeed indicator, altimeter, compass and inclinometer (which measured the aircraft's angle). To these inadequate instruments, the Smith brothers added a large helping of "seat of the pants", which comprised little more than guesswork and a sense born of experience.

At one stage they almost lost control, one moment in an

uncontrolled dive and the next approaching a stall and spin situation. Landing at Singora they came close to wrecking the aircraft when they discovered the landing strip was liberally scattered with small stumps. They had nowhere else to go, so were forced to land on the ill-prepared strip. They cleared the stumps for the next day's departure but were almost brought to grief by heavy rain. They became airborne in a spray of mud and water only a metre or so from the end of the jungle strip.

When they reached Singapore, the Australians had only four days left to reach Australia. One was used for a final check of the aircraft before setting off on the last 3800 kilometres to Darwin.

At Surabaya the aircraft bogged on landing. The thin, dry surface had cracked open, revealing a sea of mud beneath. A team of natives was organised to dig the aircraft out. Six hours later it was still stuck. The flyers were in despair. Less than 2000 kilometres from the winning post, they were hopelessly stuck, and time was running out.

Keith Smith then hit on the brainwave of having a runway constructed. Why not cover the whole take-off run with bamboo matting? The next morning an endless procession of villagers arrived carrying sheets of the matting they used to construct their houses. They were laid along the strip and the Vimy taxied gingerly over the bamboo surface. Some blew away and within seconds the aircraft was bogged again.

More mats arrived and this time a 300-metre track was laced together and pegged down. As the villagers waved and cheered, the Vimy tried again. The plane gathered speed and lifted easily into the air.

The next day they took off on the final leg of their mammoth flight, the 750-kilometre crossing of the lonely Timor Sea to Darwin. They were airborne at 8.35 a.m., again just scraping out of a short airstrip. Three hours later they passed over the cruiser HMAS *Sydney*, positioned to help if they came down in the sea. Waving sailors gave them their first taste of Australia's welcome.

At 3 p.m. on 10 December 1919, the Vickers Vimy landed at the specially constructed airfield at Fanny Bay, Darwin. One of the first to greet Ross Smith was Lieutenant Hudson Fysh (later Sir Hudson Fysh). Fysh and Lieutenant "Ginty" McGinness had slogged overland from Brisbane in a Model T Ford, establishing a chain of landing sites for the Vimy. The pair's epic overland trek would eventually lead to the formation of Australia's great international airline, Qantas, with Fysh at the helm.

Australia gave the airmen an uproarious welcome. They made a triumphant aerial tour across the country to Sydney and finally Melbourne. However, the flight across Australia was punctuated with engine and propeller problems. The Vimy was feeling the effects of the epic flight.

In Melbourne, Prime Minister Hughes presented the airmen with their cheque which the four divided equally. The Smith brothers were knighted and Shiers and Bennett given commissions.

They also heard the news that Parer and McIntosh had just left England in their battered old DH9. Even though the race was over, the pair were flying home. It took them seven months, and they virtually rebuilt the aircraft three times along the way, but "Battling Parer" and his companion finally became the second airmen to make the flight (see previous chapter).

Sir Ross Smith and his devoted mechanic, Bennett, were killed two years later while testing a new Vickers amphibian in which the brothers planned to fly around the world. His brother Keith should have been on board, but arrived late, just in time to see the aircraft enter a spin and dive into the ground. Sir Keith Smith died in 1955.

The flight of the Smith brothers in the Vimy was the first of the many great pioneering flights made by Australian airmen. Soon Bert Hinkler, Kingsford Smith and Charles Ulm would continue where the two pace-setters left off. They would fly further and faster and perhaps their feats would be better remembered by future generations than the epic flight of the Vimy. But would the nation ever again feel quite that same magic moment of pride, as it did at 3 p.m. on 10 December 1919?

In his book, *Qantas Rising*, Sir Hudson Fysh years later recalled that historic moment when Australia was first linked by air with the outside world: "It was one of the most moving sights I can remember — the termination of one of the greatest flights, if not the greatest, in the history of aviation."

6
Qantas — Born
of the Outback

Many uniquely Australian inventions have been born of
the necessity of the bush: the pedal radio, the stump-jump
plough and drizabone raincoats are a part of our heritage.
So too is Qantas, the tiny Outback air service that grew
into an international airline. Today the world's second old-
est international airline, Qantas was conceived following a
nightmare outback car journey by two Australian Flying
Corps pilots.

In 1919, when Australia's irascible Prime Minister Billy
Hughes promoted the first England — Australia air race,
Lieutenants Hudson Fysh and Paul "Ginty" McGinness
were asked to make an overland survey of the race route
between Longreach and Darwin, and arrange for the construction of airfields. Their task involved driving a wheez-
ing Model T Ford across 4000 kilometres of roadless
wilderness. Fysh and McGinness had originally been contestants in the air race until their backer had died suddenly
and they were forced to withdraw.

Sceptical locals shook their heads when, on 18 August
1919, the airmen and their driver, George Gorham, mo-
tored out of Longreach in the heavily laden Model T Ford.

They crossed the Thompson River bridge and headed
north. There were to be few bridges between there and the
Katherine River railhead near Darwin. And yet, over the
2170 kilometres of roadless wilderness that lay ahead,
they were to cross more than fifty rivers and creeks. Little
wonder the locals doubted their chances in a motor car.

Horses and camels were considered the only reliable transportation.

The Ford made good time across the Mitchell grass plains of Western Queensland and reached Cloncurry in three days. Here they had little trouble in finding a suitable site for an airfield. Before leaving they had already arranged for the aerodrome to be built at a cost of £500. It is still in regular use today.

The next leg was due north to the Gulf of Carpentaria, and they soon reached Burketown, despite a difficult river crossing. But from there on the journey became a driver's nightmare.

The locals warned them it was useless to go on. The next leg to Borroloola would be impossible in a motor vehicle.

Fysh, McGinness and Gorman decided to lighten the load on their Model T. They threw out all their tents, beds and personal gear. All that remained on board was 200 litres of petrol and water, food, spares and tools.

Against well-meaning advice they set off to cover the 650 kilometres of wilderness to Borroloola. Their route, traversed on horse by Leichhardt in 1845, was a sandy waste crisscrossed by creeks and rivers.

Soon they were to understand why the people of Burketown believed their plan was doomed to failure. River and creek crossings required hours of backbreaking work grading a track down to, and up out of, the river beds.

They repeatedly became bogged in heavy sand. Each time they had to deflate the narrow tyres and hand winch the vehicle out.

Soon they learnt to build a moving road ahead of the car with leafy branches and chicken wire. As the car passed over it they would retrieve the matting from behind and relay it on the track ahead.

At one stage they entered a 32-kilometre band of timber and cypress pine. Laboriously they felled the trees blocking their path.

The Model T soon started to show the effects of the tortuous conditions. Three times they had to remove the front axle and straighten it on a tree stump with the back of an axe. They badly damaged, but cunningly repaired, the radiator following a collision with a tree. The last days of the journey were without their radiator fan, and the engine was continually overheating.

During one particularly bad stretch of sand they were pulled along by two horses harnessed to the car. They had been bogged when miraculously they had encountered a driver who, with a spring cart and a team of twenty-eight horses, was heading for Borroloola: a fantastic stroke of luck when it is considered that the area, the size of Tasmania, had a population of fewer than a dozen white people.

On several occasions they were helped out of difficult river crossings by wandering Aborigines. These small tribal bands seemed, by their amazing "bush telegraph" to know of the journey and intercepted them in search of the much-prized white men's tobacco.

Twenty-four days after leaving Burketown they limped into Borroloola, the engine badly overheating and the damaged radiator blowing steam. There were just 12 litres of petrol remaining in the tank. They had covered 484 kilometres at an average of 24 kilometres a day, and had forded forty-six tidal rivers and creeks.

Here they rested a few days and overhauled their faithful Ford. New parts were made in the local forge from sheet iron, horseshoes and scrap wood. The work was performed by the ingenious Reverend Warren of the Roper River Mission.

They set out again on 25 September and covered the 822 kilometres to Katherine in a slow fourteen days.

Here Fysh took the weekly train, affectionately called "Leaping Lena", on to Darwin. There he chose and prepared a landing ground alongside the Fanny Bay Gaol. The whole job cost only £700. But one parliamentarian of the day called it an "utter waste of money" — so much for forward-looking politicians! Darwin today is one of Australia's busiest international airports. Meanwhile, Mc-Ginness and Gorman completed the round trip to Cloncurry in the Ford. They returned via Newcastle Waters, Brunette Downs and Camooweal, establishing three more aerodromes on the way.

Fysh remained in Darwin until the conclusion of the air race. He was the first to greet his old friend Ross Smith when he climbed out of the Vickers Vimy following its historic landing on 10 December 1919.

He left Darwin early in the New Year in another ancient Ford with a party of travellers. They followed McGinness' route back to Cloncurry.

The return journey was almost a repeat of the trials of the earlier trip. They had forty-one punctures and performed an engine overhaul en route. The inner tubes became useless and they drove kilometres with the tyres stuffed with grass. Towards the end of the trip the car broke down completely after hitting an ant-hill.

Fysh and a companion walked 112 kilometres to the next settlement and dispatched a team of horses to tow the car in for repairs.

Following their tortuous overland expedition, Fysh and McGinness realised that aeroplanes were the only practical vehicle for anyone needing to travel fast across the Outback. They were confident of finding backers for an air service following chance meetings during their journey with Fergus McMaster, the influential chairman of Cloncurry's Anti Cattle Duffing Organisation, and wealthy grazier Alexander Kennedy, who had pioneered the Cloncurry area in 1869.

In June 1920, Fysh and McGinness met with McMaster in the lounge of Brisbane's Hotel Gresham. The grazier later wrote: "They gave me an outline of a proposition for joy-flight and taxi air work in Western Queensland and the Northern Territory. I was quite prepared to assist, not only personally, but to raise sufficient capital to finance the venture.''

On 16 November 1920, Queensland and Northern Territory Aerial Services (QANTAS) was formally founded. McMaster was its first chairman and Alexander Kennedy one of its backers. Fysh and McGinness were joint managers. The company's total capital was just over £6000 – a paltry sum that today would not even cover an hour's operating costs for one of Qantas' $200-million Boeing 747-400s.

On a sizzling February afternoon in 1921, a crowd gathered on the dusty flats on the northern edge of Longreach. Out to the west, lightning flashes announced the approach of a summer storm. The red dust streets of Longreach were deserted. Everyone was at the landing ground waiting to greet "their" airline's first aeroplane.

A great cheer went up as two little biplanes landed safely. McGinness in the airline's Avro 504K was escorting a privately owned BE2, being delivered to a local citizen. Both machines looked like the other war-surplus rattletraps that barnstormed Australia in 1921. However, the tail of McGinness' Avro was emblazoned "The Queensland and N.T. Aerial Service Co Ltd. Winton". Qantas had arrived, and life in the bush would never be the same again.

Qantas' two-passenger Avro 504 had cost £1500. Within days Fysh had purchased the BE2 for a bargain-basement £450. It could only carry one passenger and was used for the joyflights – the airline's bread and butter during its first year.

With Australia still suffering from the post-war doldrums, the infant air service had to be a lean operation. Fysh and McGinness were each paid £500 per year. Besides being the only pilots they also doubled as share salesmen, traffic clerks, porters, aircraft cleaners and aerodrome rouseabouts. They gladly accepted any sort of flying to pay the bills – joyflighting, charter, even carrying airborne turkey shooters. The going rate was £1 for a ten-minute joyride and charter flights were charged at 2 shillings a mile. Fysh considered £50 for four days' outback barnstorming "a very good trip and a profitable one".

The big break came in 1922 when Qantas gained the Charleville-Cloncurry airmail contract and commenced its first regular airline service. On 22 November, flying a converted Armstrong Whitworth FK-8 bomber, McGinness left Charleville on the first stage to Longreach. On board was chief mechanic Arthur Baird and 108 letters. The second stage, to Cloncurry, was flown by Fysh, carrying their 89-year-old benefactor, Arthur Kennedy.

Passengers in today's jet airliners would be appalled at the five hours it took to the clattering biplane to complete the 480-kilometre flight. Flying commenced at daybreak and ended before the torrid heat of midday — when the underpowered biplane had trouble getting off the ground. But to Kennedy it was a miracle: the same journey had formerly taken him eight jolting months by bullock cart.

On the return flight to Charleville, Qantas carried its first real fare-paying airline passenger — 21-year-old Ivy Coates. She wrote on the pilot's log: "I was impressed with the comfort of the trip from Cloncurry and had my morning tea [from a thermos flask] speeding along at 5000 feet."

Recalling the flight during the airline's 70th birthday celebrations in 1990, 91-year-old Ivy said: "It was terribly hot on the ground but the pilot, Hudson Fysh, buttoned me up in an overcoat saying it would be cold up top. I was the only passenger and it was so noisy I had to write little notes to talk with the crew."

Her recollections also gave a perspective on the importance of that first airline service to isolated Queenslanders. She explained: "I had travelled by steamer from Brisbane to Townsville then by train to Cloncurry. It was the only way you could travel north in those days. To save time on the return journey I decided to fly from Cloncurry to Charleville then catch the train back to Brisbane."

Fysh was bitterly disappointed when his mate "Ginty" resigned. A rugged individualist, McGinness was uncomfortable with the airline routine. Things were still touch and go. Even though government subsidies eventually enabled Qantas to reduce fares by operating more economical four-passenger de Havilland DH50 planes, it still cost £21 (a month's paypacket) to fly the route between Cloncurry and Charleville. In its first twelve months of airline service, Qantas flew 204 scheduled flights and carried 156 passengers. These were the days of windblown, oil-stained pilots – and passengers. An early Qantas pilot wrote: "Considering the extreme discomfort for which they were paying, our passengers must have been in a desperate hurry to get somewhere."

Nevertheless, by 1928 Qantas was firmly established. Besides operating six DH50 biplanes, the company was also building aeroplanes at Longreach and had opened a flying school in Brisbane. It had reinforced its vital Outback role by basing a pilot and aeroplane at Cloncurry to commence the first Flying Doctor Service – a task the airline would perform until 1949.

During its years in the bush, Qantas did more than merely transport people with a need to travel far and fast. Its ubiquitous biplanes were also the pack-horses of the Outback, carrying produce and products that brightened the lives of isolated Australians.

Housewives gave their tin openers a rest when airborne deliveries of fresh vegetables broke the monotonous domination of canned food. People off the beaten track tasted fresh fish and fruit. Longreach-based pilot Russell Tapp recalled one family's delirious excitement when he delivered a case of apples to their far west property – they had not seen an apple in four years.

Qantas carried more than just staples. Bush children tasted their first icecream. After years in drab cotton, fashion-starved women bought the latest city hats and dresses. Families listened to new records, read yesterday's city paper and watched up-to-date newsreels at their local tin and canvas cinema.

Spotting fires, chasing robbers, warning of floods and searching for the missing, Qantas pilots became the eyes of the Outback. They were also the aerial iceman, news-agent, mailman and friend of isolated Australians. They became local celebrities, considered "a good catch" by husband-hunting women and hero-worshipped by children.

"Who was Pontius Pilate?" a minister asked a class at the Winton school. "He's the cove who drives the Qantas mail plane," a schoolboy answered brightly.

By 1930 the airline had extended its route west to Camooweal, north to Normanton and east from Charleville to Roma, Toowoomba and Brisbane. "Time Saved is Money Saved" extolled the Qantas timetable, illustrating how its DH50s took only two days to span the route. However, air travel was still rough and ready. Recalling the Normanton-Cloncurry section, Qantas pioneer pilot Arthur Affleck wrote:

> Passengers on this service were required to make themselves as comfortable as possible jammed into the cabin with three or four large cornsacks of wriggling, twitching fish. In addition to the two or three passengers there were suitcases, swags, saddles, rifles, mailbags, freight and a couple of savage cattle dogs travelling with their drover master. All fitted into a small, four-seater cabin. The chaos needed to be seen to be believed!

Nevertheless, the trip was remarkably fast when compared with the weeks a similar journey took by car, train and coastal steamer. Furthermore, air travel ended the total isolation the wet season frequently brought to the Outback — when floods prevented all overland travel.

In 1934, in conjunction with Britain's Imperial Airways, Qantas spread its international wings, operating the Brisbane-Singapore section of the air route to England. Renamed Qantas Empire Airways, the airline continued to service inland Queensland; however, its future growth was directed towards overseas operations. By the outbreak of the Second World War, the airline was operating its fabled Short Empire Flying Boat Service.

On 1 April 1949 the airline finally severed its last ties with the bush. Its last domestic flight, a Douglas DC-3 service from Mt Isa, landed at Brisbane's Archerfield Airport. The following day, Trans-Australia Airlines (now Australian Airlines) took over the Outback services.

Fergus McMaster years later recounted that Qantas was conceived by chance. The facts of the remarkable overland expedition certainly backed that remark. Fysh and McGinness were to have been in the 1919 Air Race, but "chance" prevented this, thus allowing them to undertake the survey trip. On this trip they realised the need for and feasibility of an air service between the remote Outback towns. It was by "chance" that McGinness should meet McMaster stranded outside Cloncurry. A gesture of Outback hospitality brought about the "chance" meeting with Alexander Kennedy.

Two disappointed airmen drove out of Longreach in 1919 into the wilderness. When they returned they had not only overcome the "impossible", but had also laid the foundations of Australia's great international airline.

7
Outback Pioneer

Late in the afternoon of 22 April 1918, six Australian Flying Corps officers stood around a grave in a small French cemetery. On a word from the chaplain they lowered a simple coffin as a firing party of bush-hatted Australian soldiers fired three volleys into the air. The coffin had nearly reached the grave bottom when one of the airmen slipped as soil at the edge of the grave crumbled away. He was prevented from falling in only by the quick grasp of a fellow officer.

Thus it was that Australian pioneer airman Jack Treacy, a First World War pilot with the Australian Flying Corps' No. 3 Squadron, nearly became the man who went to the grave with Baron von Richthofen — the dreaded Red Baron — the most famous fighter ace of all time.

Jack Treacy outlived his foe to enjoy his retirement at Yamba in northern New South Wales. His flying career, which spanned forty years, saw Australian aviation grow from a few ramshackle, war-disposal aircraft to today's great airline and general aviation industry.

He was not one of the record-breaking pioneers in the mould of Hinkler, Smithy or Ulm, but was one of a larger band of the unsung heroes of Australian aviation: the men who quietly went their way setting up the tiny bush airlines and flying schools — the one-man-one-plane businesses that helped develop of our modern aviation industry.

Jack was born in Wagga in 1895. His father, a one time world champion pigeon shooter, encouraged his son to take up engineering and had him apprenticed to a Sydney company.

He completed his apprenticeship as the First World War broke out and enlisted straight away as a mechanic in the AFC. In 1915 he was sent to England and placed in charge of a Royal Flying Corps mobile workshop and soon he had the flying bug. (Not content to work on aircraft, he wanted to become a pilot and head for the action.) Three months later he was accepted into the cadet school at Reading for elementary pilot training from where he went to No.66 Training Squadron at Yatesbury. He received his pilot wings after a very skimpy flying course conducted on several different types of early RFC. With less than ten hours solo flying in his pilot logbook he was sent to France to face the then better equipped German Air Force.

It was early 1917 and the average life expectancy of Allied pilots was around five weeks. By "Bloody April 1917" the Germans had achieved complete air superiority on the Western Front. Their Fokker and Albatros fighters could outrun, outmanoeuvre and outgun the RFC's obsolete machines.

Jack Treacy was posted to the Australian No. 3 Squadron to fly RE8 two-seater, general-purpose aircraft. They were mainly used for reconnaissance, artillery spotting, photography and occasional ineffective bombing missions. Known to their pilots as "Harry Tates", after a British music-hall comedian (maybe because their performance was a bit of a laugh), the lumbering RE8s suffered terrible losses — especially to the newly formed Richthofen Flying Circus. So poor was their performance that the Germans considered them the ideal "easy meat" for newly arrived fighter pilots to cut their teeth on. The Harry Tates were also noted as "flamers" because they almost always seemed to catch on fire when hit, giving their non-parachute-equipped crews no chance to escape a terrible death. Crews were often seen to jump to their death thousands of feet up, rather than face an agonising end by fire.

Jack Treacy was one of the lucky few. He survived for 200 hours of flying those death traps over enemy lines and crossed the front on 110 missions, conducting aerial photographic surveys of enemy installations and trenches (his logbook records that he brought back 140 photographs of military targets). He also completed bombing and artillery observation missions and was attacked on numerous occasions, but was never shot down.

On 6 June 1917 he had a close call. Treacy had taken off at dawn on an artillery spotting flight because heavy enemy artillery fire had been playing havoc with the entrenched Australian Corps diggers in the Bayonsvilliers-Bray sector of the front. His job was to locate the German battery and direct Allied artillery fire on the enemy position.

By 5.30 a.m. the RE8 was near the town of Dernancourt and had fixed the enemy position. Observer Lieutenant N.H. Jones was recording the map co-ordinates while Treacy circled over the enemy battery. It was time-consuming work, requiring a high degree of concentration from both men, and while their attention was directed to the ground, an enemy Albatros Scout crept up on the unsuspecting Australians.

The first warning they had was the rattle of machine gun fire as the German fighter came up under their tail. Treacy yanked the lumbering observation plane into a tight turn while Observer Jones dropped his maps and grabbed his Lewis gun.

Both men realised their position was desperate. A lone aircraft, well behind enemy lines and with no chance of outrunning their speedier and more heavily armed attacker, their only hope it seemed was to try and out-turn the Albatros and hope that its pilot would not inflict fatal damage before he ran out of ammunition.

With the control stick hard back and using full power, Treacy held the aircraft through turn after turn. For once the RE8's lack of speed was an advantage – it enabled the aircraft to fly a tighter circle than its German aggressor and avoid being hit. But the Australians knew it was only a matter of time before the German pilot would change his attack tactics and himself slow down and lock in behind their tail.

Treacy decided to go on the offensive. He was able to get in several wild bursts of fire with his forward-firing Vickers gun. Jones also let loose several long bursts from the rear cockpit. They did not hit the enemy fighter but nevertheless their efforts had a remarkable effect: as though scared by such determined and unexpected resistance, the enemy pilot pulled out of the fight. And then, to the Australians' complete amazement, he peeled away and headed for home.

The Albatros pilot must have been a raw novice not to have realised that had he used the correct tactics the unescorted RE8 was a sitting duck. He had only to wait for the right moment and Treacy would have had no chance against the superior performance of the enemy aircraft. Treacy's combat report was one of a number of similar accounts made by 3 Squadron pilots recording the disinclination of some German pilots to press home their attack when met by determined resistance.

In August of that year, Jack Treacy took part in an operation which demonstrated the versatility of the aircraft as a war machine. Not a bullet was fired, not an explosive bomb dropped, yet four of 3 Squadron's aircraft were responsible for saving countless lives.

In the battle for the Somme, the Australian 1st Division were ordered to attack on the left flank and advance in stages to the outskirts of Cachy. The ground over which the diggers were to advance was directly under the guns of the enemy artillery on high ground nearby, and for the Australian infantry to cross the open ground unsupported would have been suicidal.

The answer to the problem came from the RE8s of the AFC. Treacy led three other aircraft piloted by Lieutenants K. Roberts, H. Foale and D. Dimsey over the area. It was just on dawn and the diggers were due to leave their trenches within minutes.

The four aircraft swept low in front of the German positions, dropping a succession of smoke bombs and within a minute a dense screen covered the area. Their timing was perfect. At 4.45 a.m. precisely, the order to attack passed along the lines and a sea of khaki figures climbed out of the trenches into no man's land. Thanks to the efforts of the Australian airmen, the advance was hidden from the German guns so that by the time they finally sighted the charging diggers it was too late. By 8 a.m., No. 3 Squadron observation aircraft reported that the enemy positions had been taken. Casualties had been light.

The Australians were working the sector around the Somme which was the hunting ground of Richthofen's Jasta 11. Many of their losses had been at the hands of the Baron's group of gaudily painted Fokkers. On the day the Red Baron was killed, he led his Fokkers on to a formation of two No. 3 Squadron RE8s, but for once they were unable to make the "kill". The two pilots, Lieutenants Simpson and Garrett, like Jack Treacy, had learned the art of defensive survival.

By flying in tight circles, each defending the other's tail, they were able to survive until a flight of Sopwith Camels came to their aid; in fact, they even shot down one of Richthofen's formation. The arrival of the Camels, commanded by Canadian Captain Roy Brown, led to a chain of events that ended with Richthofen's Fokker Triplane crashing in front of the Allied lines at Corbie Hill, starting a controversy that remains today.

Jack Treacy was not sure who shot him down, but he was positive that it was not Roy Brown's Camel. "It was definitely a machine gunner on the ground," he recalled. "From the position the bullet entered and then exited the Baron's body there is no way it came from Brown's aircraft.

"I think it is likely that the machine gunner was Gunner Buie. However, there were a number of others it might have been. Every one around claimed him except the WAACs (Womens Army Air Corps) and the Chinese Labour Battalion."

The body of the German ace was taken to No. 3 Squadron's base at Poulainville. It was laid on a sheet of galvanised iron in the tent hangar which normally housed Jack Treacy's RE8. Besides conducting an autopsy, the authorities called for official photographs to be taken of the Baron's body. While Sergeant John Alexander, the official No. 3 Squadron AFC photographer, took pictures of the body, several squadron pilots were in attendance and Jack Treacy was one of them. He had brought along his own pocket camera, but noticing the terrible bruising and cuts on the dead German's face he suggested that some sort of powder should be used to whiten the battered features. Jack found some baking powder which he applied to the wounds and then he and Sergeant Alexander took their grisly pictures.

An often-published picture of the Baron in death clearly shows traces of the baking powder on the lapels of the German's flying coat.

"He was a good pilot and, of course, he was famed for his 80 victories, but I don't really know why he became a legend," said Jack. "We had good pilots, too, Mannock brought down early 80, the Canadian Bishop over 70 and the Frenchman Fonck shot down 75."

The point that Jack Treacy made is quite understandable, but probably the key to the Baron's immortality lies not with his fame in life but with the controversy surrounding his death. It carried on for decades and is still argued today by the oldtimers. It was the mystery and the wild claims about who fired the fatal bullet that sparked scores of books and hundreds of articles on the German ace. It is now generally accepted that Gunners Popkin and Weston of the 24th Machine Gun Company, Fourth Australian Division, were the unsung heroes.

As 1917 went by, Jack became one of the "old hands": he had survived the critical period of inexperience. By the end of the year he had amassed the total sixty hours' flying time — not much by modern standards, but a lifetime on the Western Front.

It seems that the macabre moments are often those that are best recalled years later — like the particular flight when he was spotting for, and directing the fire of, a British heavy gun battery. The target was a battery of German artillery entrenched behind the lines near the village of Albert. The enemy fire was being directed from an observation post in a tall tower and it was causing havoc in the mud-filled Allied trenches.

Treacy circled the area until his observer fixed the enemy position and signalled the map co-ordinates to their 8-inch howitzer battery. All the time the Australian pilot was anxiously scanning the skies for German fighters, but they were lucky and none came.

When the howitzers opened fire they were spot on target. As the airmen watched, a shell fell right into one of the German gun pits and the explosion blew the gun and its luckless crew right out of the pit. The gun and "rag doll" crew lifted into the air, turning over and over before falling back to the ground above the shattered gun emplacement.

By mid-1918 the Sopwith Camels and SE5 fighters of the Royal Flying Corps had regained air superiority and the murderous losses of the observation aircraft had decreased.

Jack was witness to one of the most unusual actions involving a No. 3 Squadron pilot. A Captain Armstrong was airborne on a spotting mission when he closed on to a German Albatros single-seater on the Allied side of the trenches. As the Australian positioned for an attack, he was dumbfounded to see his enemy raise his hands in a signal of surrender. Suspecting a trap, he slowly and carefully manoeuvred to a position in close formation beside and slightly astern of the Albatros: there he was clear of the enemy's field of fire and well placed to recommence his attack if the German was playing some trick.

Armstrong then pointed in the direction of his home base and shepherded the German back for a landing. Australian ground crew and off-duty pilots stared in disbelief as the unlikely formation arrived overhead and landed.

A strange code of honour existing among the First World War airmen. It was almost a game. "The Huns are really good chaps − good sports and all that stuff," they said. Thus the downed German was invited to the Officers' Mess for a meal and drinks with all the Squadron pilots.

"He thought the guard that marched him over to our mess might have been a firing squad. It took quite a while before he relaxed and understood that we were honouring him as a fellow airman. He told us he had flown too low behind our lines, got lost, and was afraid that he had no hope of getting back through our ground and air defences."

A month before the war ended, Jack was finally rested from action when he was posted to England as a ferry pilot. Following the Armistice in November 1918 he took a job with the Bristol-based British and Colonial Aeroplane Company working under F.S. Barnwell, the brilliant designer of the highly successful Bristol Fighter. There Jack's earlier engineering training was enhanced by experience in the skills of aircraft design and construction.

By December 1919 he had returned to Australia complete with an English war bride.

In the early years of peace he turned his hand to just about every type of flying job that was going. It was hard to make a living: he was just one of a flood of ex-wartime pilots all trying to turn their military skills into a civilian career. Joyriding, passenger flying, barnstorming, instructing − they tried anything to pay the bills and keep flying.

For a while he flew with the fledgling Australian Aircraft and Engineering Company started by Harry Broad-

smith, a former engineer with A.V. Roe-England. The pilots did all manner of jobs but the money was in joyriding
the thousands of Australians who wanted a taste of flying.
In 1920, during the two-week Brisbane Show, the company took in £3000 from ten-minute flips over Brisbane's
Eagle Farm Racecourse. In those days that was a small
fortune that would probably equal $60 000 today.

Jack Treacy made headlines when he delivered an Avro
Sunbeam Dyak from the company's newly purchased
Mascot airfield and factory to P. Hogarth of Richmond in
North Queensland. The 2900-kilometre flight established
a long-distance record for the delivery flight of a civil air-
craft.

He became Australia's "Flying Picture Show Man"
when he was contracted to Fox Films — with the 1920s the
movies had become big business. Every little Outback
town had a cinema, but often it was only a tin shed or rows
of canvas chairs under the stars.

Day after day Jack flew from town to town delivering
and picking up the cans of precious film. He crisscrossed
New South Wales and Queensland a score of times. There
were no aerodromes — at best it was a local racecourse or
a clear paddock and often it was a bush track or a salt pan
with no wind socks to help pick the landing direction. Jack
learned to read the wind by observing washing on a back-
yard line, ripples on a nearby creek or smoke from a
bushfire. These were real "seat of the pants" flying days.

Often he would do a bit of stunt flying to help with advertising and promoting films. On one such occasion he
was looping the loop for a race crowd at Brisbane's Eagle
Farm track. He had a passenger on board — his 2-year-old
daughter whom, he believed, held a world record for hours
in the air for any child. She was strapped tightly in the
cockpit as he pulled the aircraft around on its back at the
top of the loop. Suddenly a large cushion tumbled out of
the open cockpit and plummeted down towards the
ground. The huge crowd gasped in terror and then sighed

with relief when they realised the falling object was not the child. Perhaps it was showmanship? It was the era of the spine-chilling barnstormers.

In 1921 he became the first man to land on the site of today's Eagle Farm Airport at Brisbane – when it was a dairy farm. He advised the newly formed Civil Aviation Department that it would make an ideal landing ground.

In the same year, Australia's greatest solo record breaker, Bert Hinkler, had brought his tiny Avro "Baby" biplane from England. He had hoped to fly here but had been stopped in Italy by a Middle East war, so he and his Avro had arrived by sea. During an aerial tour of the country, Hinkler severely damaged the aircraft landing on a windswept New South Wales beach. Hinkler sold the wreck and returned to England, but Jack Treacy was asked to help rebuild the unique machine and was later allocated the Avro for film-delivery flying. He took it all over the country.

The Civil Aviation Department was getting organised and required all pilots to be tested and licensed. They issued him Commercial Pilot Licence No. 23 and he also received an aircraft engineer's licence.

Jack recalled the early days of Brisbane's Archerfield Aerodrome:

> It was not an ideal site. The drome sloped away and you were either taking off uphill or downhill. There were a lot of chicken farms around it and one farmer in particular was irate at all the noise. He swore it put his hens off laying. He used to get a gun out and take pot shots at aircraft flying over his property.

The hard and often frustrating years of barnstorming and bush flying finally paid off when, in 1928, he was appointed Chief Pilot of the newly formed Queensland Air Navigation Ltd. Flying tri-motored Fokker Airliners, similar to Smithy's *Southern Cross*, the fledgling airline linked Brisbane, Rockhampton and Townsville with their first regular air service.

Jack made the inaugural flight to Townsville. He said:

By modern standards we had no real navigation equipment on those old Fokkers. We flew by compass alone. They only had primitive blind flying instruments and flying in cloud was really flying "blind". On the six-hour flights during the cyclone season we were usually in cloud for four or five hours.

A beautifully preserved wooden propeller from one of those Fokkers has pride of place on the wall of the Townsville Aero Club.

But the hard times were not yet over. In the early days it was touch and go whether the airline would survive. Like many of the first airlines, QAN used every aerial trick of the trade to get people into the air and keep funds rolling in. The company established a flying school at Townsville where for £4 18s North Queensland's budding pilots got an hour's dual flying with company instructor Jim Branch.

One of their first students was 17-year-old Post Office employee Bob Brown. Months before, Brown had written away for the plans of a Heath Super Parasol light aircraft. In a shed near his Home Hill home, he was busy building his own plane and dreamed of one day flying the miniaircraft. He had taken a joyride with Jim Branch and then signed up for a course of training. After only his first lesson he was informed that he was due for a check flight with the company's "Chief Pilot and technical adviser" who was flying up specially from Brisbane to check all the Townsville students. Next day Jack Treacy arrived on the scene.

"There were only half a dozen pupils and Jack said he wanted to fly with each of us," Brown recalled forty years later. "I got into the back seat not knowing just what to expect. He had taken a quarter-hour ticket from me first. That was worth £1 4s 6d — a lot of money in those days.

"I didn't do much of the flying at all. With only one lesson under my belt I didn't know much about what was going on. He did some very steep turns and the landing.

No way could you have called it a check or even instruction."

It was probably a bit of a con job, but every little helped in the early days when flying was a hand-to-mouth existence and next week's payroll had to be met somehow. Bob continued his training and finally soloed in his home-built aircraft which he grandly named *Spirit of Aussie*.

In another promotional and fund-raising effort, Treacy visited small towns in the company's Avro Sunbeam Dyak dressed in a distinctive flying outfit. He would place advertisements in the local papers and pin up posters advertising joyflights. "Flights 10/-. Look for the man in grey" they announced.

His long flying career included a stint of bush flying in New Guinea, where he operated a two-seat biplane, carrying passengers and cargo in and out of the treacherous highlands. He considered it the most dangerous assignment of his life. The country's mountains, clouds and eagle-perch airstrips took a terrible toll on the unwary or inexperienced pilot. Jack believed that those who survived a New Guinea baptism became some of the world's best pilots.

He made his last flight in 1952. At the age of 57 he decided it was time to hang up his wings.

In 1978 he was an honoured guest of the Australian government at the celebrations to commemorate the fiftieth anniversary of the crossing of the Pacific by Smithy, Ulm and the crew of the *Southern Cross*. Seated among the handful of Australia's surviving early birds, Jack watched as Charles Kingsford Smith, Jr. landed at Brisbane's Eagle Farm Airport after retracing his famous father's flight.

The Eagle Farm he saw was vastly different from the dairy farm on which he had been the first to land. When the official celebrations were over, Jack and his close friend and travelling companion Syd Wilson joined the crowd around Smithy's *Southern Cross* memorial. He no doubt recalled the hundreds of hours he spent at the controls of a similar machine punching through the storms to Townsville.

But the most memorable moment of his two-day visit came when Jack attended a function at the Queensland Museum. He and Syd had moved away from the admirers surrounding Smithy, Jnr. and his mother (the former Lady Kingsford Smith). Slowly they walked down to the far end of the museum. Above Jack's head hung Bert Hinkler's restored Avro Baby, the same aircraft he had rebuilt and flown for Fox Films.

There was a faraway look and just the hint of a tear in his eyes. It was as if the memory-dimming veil of fifty-seven years had dropped away. He and the little Baby were again airborne battling the dust, dodging the storms and heading west for the setting sun and some tiny Outback town. Stowed in the tiny open cockpit were the precious cans of film which would that night bring entertainment and the world to the isolated bush people — to them he was the flying-picture-show-man who somehow always managed to get through.

To those Australians, men like Jack Treacy were the real aviation pioneers.

8
Across the Top
of the World

In 1958, the United States Navy nuclear submarine *Skate* surfaced slowly through an opening in the ice cap close to the North Pole. The ensign was lowered and the crew assembled at attention. To the sound of the Last Post and a ceremonial volley of rifle fire, the ashes of Sir Hubert Wilkins, Australia's greatest polar explorer, were scattered over the vast frozen waste where he had spent much of his life.

Few Australians have been held in such high esteem throughout the world as this great airman-explorer who ranked with Amundsen, Shackleton, Byrd, Stefansson and Scott, the other great explorers of the polar regions. Photographer, explorer, airman . . . Sir Hubert was an expert in each field. His story has almost been forgotten. Yet in 1928 his name was on the front pages of newspapers around the world. In April of that year, accompanied by an American pilot, he navigated his single-engined monoplane from America to Europe across the Arctic ice cap. Thus he pioneered the polar route flown by many of today's big jets.

George Hubert Wilkins was born on Mount Bryan East station in South Australia. As a young boy he always had his nose in a book, preferring stories of adventure and exploration. His inquiring mind also turned to astronomy and meteorology. The station was enduring one of the worst droughts in living memory. Though still only a boy, he devised a system of weather recording and long-range fore-

HOUDINI PILOTING HIS VOISIN BIPLANE. THE FIRST SUCCESSFUL AVIATOR IN AUSTRALIA. WINS THE AUSTRALIAN AERO LEAGUE'S TROPHY, MARCH 15th, 1910. MELBOURNE, AUSTRALIA.

Harry Houdini (inset) takes off from Digger's Rest, Victoria, on his first flight on 18 March 1910 (not the 15th as recorded on the original caption) (Courtesy Smithsonian Institution, National Air and Space Museum)

Houdini (third from left) talks to onlookers shortly before making his first flight at Digger's Rest, Victoria (Courtesy Smithsonian Institution, National Air and Space Museum)

John Duigan in flight over Mia Mia, Victoria, in the first Australian-built aeroplane (Courtesy Science Museum of Victoria)

Captain Robert Alexander Little, DSO & Bar, DSC & Two Bars, Croix de Guerre – the top-scoring Australian fighter ace

A Royal Naval Air Service Maurice Farman Longhorn trainer, the type flown by Little in 1916. To touch the only set of controls the pupil (seated rear) had to lean forward and reach around the instructor's shoulders.

Sopwith's deadly Triplane. Captain Little and the revolutionary fighter were a deadly combination – he recorded 33 kills in this type in just four months. (Courtesy Smithsonian Institution, National Air and Space Museum)

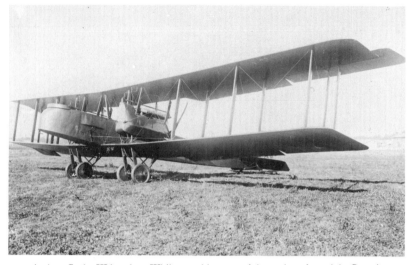

A giant Gotha III bomber. While attacking one of these aircraft at night Captain Little lost his life. (Courtesy Smithsonian Institution, National Air and Space Museum)

By shooting down through a tunnel in the fuselage, the tail gunner of the Gotha III was able to fire at approaching aircraft from below the tailplane area (Courtesy Smithsonian Institution, National Air and Space Museum)

Harry Hawker pictured with a Morane Saulnier Scout Type H monoplane (Courtesy Smithsonian Institution, National Air and Space Museum)

Thomas Sopwith (left), Harry Hawker, and the two-seater Tabloid Hawker demonstrated in Australia in 1914. In the same year a float-equipped Tabloid won the Schneider Trophy race. (Courtesy Smithsonian Institution, National Air and Space Museum)

Hawker's Sopwith Atlantic, powered by a 350 horsepower Rolls-Royce Eagle engine, could carry 1,800 litres of fuel. It featured jettisonable landing gear and on top of the fuselage from the rear cockpit to the tailplane was a detachable boat. (Courtesy Smithsonian Institution, National Air and Space Museum)

Several days after Hawker's mid-Atlantic rescue a French ship found the semi-submerged remains of the Sopwith and took it on board (Courtesy Smithsonian Institution, National Air and Space Museum)

Lieutenants Ray Parer (right) and John McIntosh and the de Havilland DH9 just before leaving Hounslow Aerodrome, London on their heroic journey (Courtesy Queensland Newspapers)

Parer and McIntosh refuelling *P.D.* at Longreach. The two automobile radiators fitted in Burma can be seen hanging beneath the fuselage — just ahead of the landing gear. (Author's collection)

Following its final mishap near Albury, the battered *P.D.* was transported over-land to Flemington Racecourse for Melbourne's welcome home ceremony for the two airman (Courtesy Queensland Newspapers)

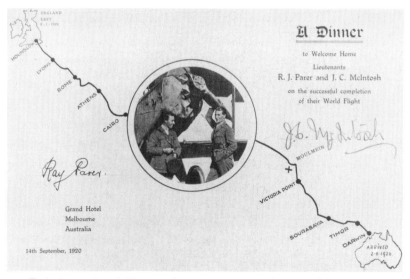

Both airmen signed this souvenir menu commemorating a special celebratory dinner given them at Melbourne's Grand Hotel (Courtesy M. Parer)

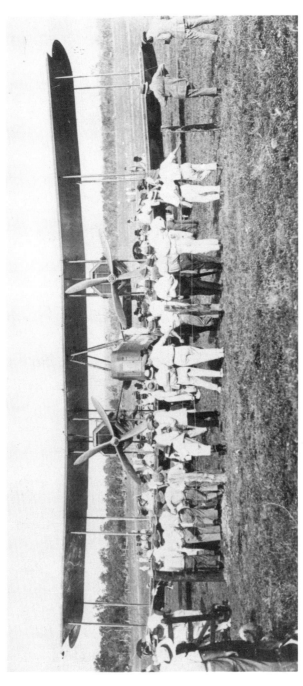

The Vickers Vimy G-EAOU at Darwin's Fanny Bay Airfield on 10 December 1919 following its pioneering flight from England (Source unknown – author's collection)

The crew of the Vickers Vimy G-EAOU pictured at the Darwin home of the Northern Territory Administrator, the Honorable Stainforth Smith (in white), are (left to right): Sgts Jim Bennett and Wally Shiers, Capt Ross Smith, Lt Hudson Fysh and Lt Keith Smith. Lt Fysh organised the building of the Fanny Bay Airport. (Courtesy Queensland Newspapers)

In 1919 fuel pumps and bowsers were unknown in Australia. The Vickers Vimy G-EAOU had to be hand-filled from petrol cans. A task made more arduous as each drop of fuel had to be filtered through shammy leather to keep out dust and water. (Courtesy Queensland Newspapers)

In recognition of the 1919 England-Australia flight, Charleville produced this special montage depicting the crew, aircraft and route they flew (Courtesy Queensland Newspapers)

Photograph taken by Lt Hudson Fysh during the epic overland air route survey. Aboriginal stockmen help the airmen negotiate a dry river bed in their Ford Model T. (Courtesy Qantas)

Hudson Fysh (left) and engineer Arthur Baird with the Qantas BE 2E. In 1921 this war-surplus plane and an Avro 504 formed the airline's total fleet. (Courtesy Qantas)

(Top) In 1990 nonagenarians Jack Haslett and Ivy Coates met in Brisbane to recall the day (in the lower picture) when they made history. In November 1922, pictured with pilot Paul McGinness (right) and engineer Jack Haslett, Ivy Coates flew on the return leg of Qantas' first scheduled airline service – between Charleville and Cloncurry. Issued ticket No. 2, she was the first woman passenger – and arguably the first real fare-paying passenger. (Courtesy Qantas)

Qantas — 1930 as depicted by a promotional display card (Courtesy Qantas)

In 1932 the airline's 14-plane fleet comprised exclusively de Havilland aircraft. Here outside the Qantas hangar at Brisbane's Archerfield Airport are: (left to right) a pair of DH 60 Moths, DH 80 Puss Moth, DH 61 Giant Moth and a DH 50J (Courtesy Qantas)

Capt. Jack Treacy, Australian Flying Corps 1918 (Courtesy Jack Treacy)

The burial of Baron von Richthofen. At right Jack Treacy bends low over the foot of the German ace's coffin. (Courtesy Duxford Air Museum)

An RE 8 of No. 3 Squadron AFC. In this lumbering fire trap Treacy survived 200 hours flying over the Western Front. (Courtesy Australian War Memorial)

In 1921 Treacy, pictured here with his brother and father, was flying this tiny Avro Baby formerly owned by Bert Hinkler (Courtesy Jack Treacy)

The *Star of Townsville* with Captain Jack Treacy at the controls, arrives at Townsville on its inaugural flight on 31 March 1931 (Courtesy Australia Post)

Hubert Wilkins (holding a compass) and his pilot Carl Ben Eielson at Point Barrow prior to their transpolar flight (Courtesy Smithsonian Institution, National Air and Space Museum)

Wilkins and Eielson flew a ski-equipped version of Lockheed's successful Vega monoplane (here seen in its normal wheeled configuration) (Courtesy Smithsonian Institution, National Air and Space Museum)

In 1931 Wilkins climbed down the hatch of an old US Navy submarine he named *Nautilus* and attempted to sail under the North Pole (Courtesy Adelaide *Advertiser*)

Australia's quiet hero Bert Hinkler (Courtesy Amalgamated Press Ltd)

Pictured with his beloved Avro Avian, Hinkler was an enigma in an era of flamboyant aviation heroes. In business suit and tie, with a minimum of fuss, he quietly bridged the continents. (Courtesy Queensland Newspapers)

During his triumphant Australian tour Hinkler was accompanied by his wife Nancy on the eastbound flight from Perth. Here (probably at Kalgoorlie) they are greeted by locals. (Source unknown)

Following his 1928 solo flight from England, the streets of Brisbane were jammed as Hinkler and his Avro Avian were paraded through the city (Courtesy Queensland Newspapers)

Jessie "Chubbie" Miller photographed in the USA shortly before she competed in the 1929 National Air Races (Courtesy Smithsonian Institution, National Air and Space Museum)

Chubbie Miller made headlines in 1927 when she became the first woman to fly from England to Australia as a passenger in Captain Bill Lancaster's Avro Avian *Red Rose* (Courtesy Queensland Newspapers)

Flanked by aircraft builder Sherman Fairchild (right) and his pilot Bob Rearkirt, the diminutive Chubbie Miller takes delivery of the Fairchild F.34 she flew in the 1929 National Air Tour. Both her aircraft and stylish flying gear were white with black trim. (Courtesy Smithsonian Institution, National Air and Space Museum)

Chubbie Miller in the cockpit of her Fairchild (Coutesy Smithsonian Institution, National Air and Space Museum)

The remains of Bill Lancaster and his *Southern Cross Minor* found in the Sahara in 1962 by a French Army patrol (Courtesy Smithsonian Institution, National Air and Space Museum)

Francis Chichester and his float-equipped de Havilland DH60 Gipsy Moth *Madame Elijah* (Author's collection)

Chichester's *Madame Elijah* is lifted from the sea to the jetty at Norfolk Island's Cascade Bay (Courtesy Queensland Newspapers)

Lord Howe Islanders helped drag *Madame Elijah* to the beach after it overturned and was submerged at its moorings during a violent storm (Author's collection)

Chichester (on ladder) rebuilt *Madame Elijah* with the help of Lord Howe Islanders (Author's collection)

Miraculously Chichester survived when his Gipsy Moth crashed into the sea wall at Katsuura, Japan (Courtesy Queensland Newspapers)

"You might make it if you've got the guts," Charles Kingsford Smith told Lores Bonney before her around-Australia flight in 1932 (Courtesy Lores Bonney)

Lores Bonney flying around Australia in 1932 in her de Havilland DH60 Gipsy Moth *My Little Ship* (Courtesy Lores Bonney)

A lone spectator watches as a photographer records Lores Bonney's arrival at London's Croydon Airport in 1932. (Note the spare propeller strapped to her aircraft.) (Courtesy Lores Bonney)

The take-off accident at Livingstone that almost ended Lores Bonney's Cape Town flight (Courtesy Lores Bonney)

Willing hands assist the local blacksmith make repairs at Livingston to Lores Bonney's Klemm monoplane. Lores (with hand on cowling) helps put weight on the plank supporting her damaged aircraft. (Courtesy Lores Bonney)

In 1981 Queensland pilot/schoolteacher Dorothy Dean (holding flowers) recreated Lores Bonney's around Australia flight. Among those welcoming her back in Brisbane were her hero Lores (centre) and Elaine Darling MHR (left) (Author's collection)

Sidney Cotton and his de Havilland DH14A at Hendon shortly before the start of the 1920 London-Cape Town Challenge (Courtesy Vera Cotton)

Cotton's de Havilland DH4 fitted with his own innovation, twin upward-firing Lewis guns for attacking Zeppelins. He had his aircraft camouflaged – an idea later adopted by the Royal Flying Corps. (Courtesy Vera Cotton)

Cotton's ski-equipped Westland Limousine III on the ice at Botwood, Newfoundland in 1922. He pioneered aerial spotting for Canadian sealers and fishermen. (Courtesy Vera Cotton)

Sidney Cotton's sister Vera (seated) and wife Bunty and his Lockheed 12A *Caprice* – similar to the Lockheed he used on clandestine photographic missions over Germany (Courtesy Vera Cotton)

Sidney Cotton during World War II (Courtesy Vera Cotton)

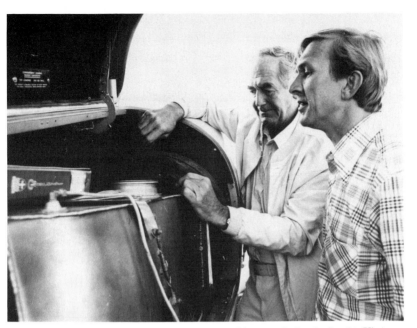

Denys Dalton (left) and the author inspect one of the extra fuel tanks fitted to Victor-Kilo Echo for their around-the-world flight (Courtesy Queensland Newspapers)

Denys Dalton's record-breaking Beechcraft B-60 Duke VH-TKE – *Duke of Broadbeach* – now hangs in the Queensland Museum (Author's collection)

Dalton's storm-scarred Duke taxies into its Coolangatta home base with the new world record on 26 July 1975. On its hail punctured nose can be seen the metal bandage provided by British Airways at Dubai. (Courtesy Queensland Newspapers)

The moment of relief. The airmen's wives had little sleep waiting for cables from around the world marking the Duke's progress. From left: Patrick Gwynn-Jones, the author and his wife Susan, and Norma and Denys Dalton. (Courtesy Queensland Newspapers)

casting to prepare for future droughts; many years later, scientists perfected a similar scheme.

At the age of 16 he went to the Adelaide School of Mines where he found the technical education both stimulating and challenging. A holiday visit to a Sydney cinema led to his first occupation. He decided to become a movie cameraman, but for this he had to go overseas. In England he devoted all his energies to becoming one of the best cine and still photographers of Europe. He also became swept up in the craze of flying that had hit America and Europe following the Wright brothers' first flight in 1903.

By 1912 the 24-year-old photographer was an accomplished pilot close to receiving his licence, when war broke out in the Balkans. Within days he was on his way to Turkey to take film and act as correspondent for a British newspaper. Determined to get photos and a story from the very heart of the battle zone, Wilkins persuaded a Turkish pilot to fly him right over the front lines. Although the pilot was officially credited with the flight, the first over a battle, Wilkins in fact did the flying!

The Turkish authorities, however, took a dim view of his escapade. Unable to believe that a war correspondent would subject himself to such danger just to get a story, they decided he must be an enemy spy. The young Australian was arrested and sentenced to death by firing squad. He was one of a line of men awaiting execution, and several had already been shot, when an interpreter arrived and Wilkins was reprieved. He took the whole thing quite calmly, recounting that he never really believed they would fire when his turn came!

Returning to England he was given the job of editing films that had been taken during Shackleton and Scott's expeditions to the poles. His imagination fired by these earliest films of the great unexplored wastelands, Wilkins decided to go to the Arctic. There he met Vilhjalmur Stefansson, the great Icelandic explorer/scientist, whose combined ideas of exploration and scientific research appealed to the Australian's technical yet adventurous nature. He joined the Icelander and in three years received a schooling in Arctic travel and survival that became the basis of all his future explorations. Stefansson firmly believed that to survive in the Arctic one had to learn to live like the Eskimos. The wandering native tribes travelled the barren ice with a minimum of food and equipment. Their principle of travelling light and fishing and hunting for food was, in Stefansson's opinion, the only solution for satisfactory exploration.

Wilkins accompanied his Icelandic tutor on a harrowing expedition to the Canadian Arctic Islands, where he displayed the courage and determination that was to become the hallmark of his future adventures. One by one, the other members of the expedition dropped out until the young Australian was the only companion left with Stefansson. Despite severe snowblindness and frostbite, he did not give up. It was on this trip that Wilkins first dreamed of using an aircraft to explore the icelands. "I did not enjoy running after the dog sleds. I found it hard on the feet. I used to imagine I was sailing along in an aeroplane with the broad panorama of ice beneath me," he wrote. He reckoned that even the crude aircraft of that time could cover in one day what it took a man and dog sled twelve days to survey.

He returned to England to find the world at war. He immediately joined the Australian Flying Corps, but was turned down for pilot training because of defective eyesight, a legacy from his recent snowblindness. However, his skills with the camera were noted and he was appointed as official photographer to the Australian Imperial Force in France. His courage and leadership in the field were proved on several occasions when he took command of troops whose officers had been killed in action. His acts of gallantry won him a Military Cross.

Another challenge presented itself soon after the Armistice, when Wilkins was introduced to the crew of the

Blackburn Kangaroo. They were desperately searching for a navigator to get them back to Australia in the great 1919 Air Race. But the flight ended when an engine blew up near Crete. Following the unsuccessful Kangaroo adventure, Wilkins attempted to mount a transpolar airship flight, but was unable to raise the necessary funds. He took part in several expeditions, including a scientific survey of northern Australia. But the Arctic still fascinated him.

Finally the American Geographic Society and the *Detroit News* came to his rescue. Between them they put up sufficient funds for his planned exploration and survey of the Arctic by aeroplane. The experts said it could not be done. Aircraft were too unreliable and risky to use in the sub-zero wilderness. They recalled the disappearance of Dr Andree's balloon expedition. But the Australian was adamant that the aircraft was the explorer's tool of the future. Point Barrow in Alaska was his choice as the base for the Arctic flights. From the Fokker Aircraft Company he purchased two monoplanes: one powered by a single Liberty engine he named *Alaskan*, the other a similar type but with three motors he christened *Detroiter* in honour of his backers. They were considered the best aircraft of their time. The chief pilot of the expedition was a United States Army pilot, Lt Carl Eielson. A young American of Norwegian descent, he had considerable experience of flying in Alaska.

In temperatures of minus 10⁰C they attempted to commence operations with the Fokkers. But crash followed crash. In one day Wilkins survived two crashes with different pilots. Tragedy struck a few days later when Palmer Hutchison, the expedition's press agent, walked into a spinning propeller and died instantly. Nevertheless enough flights had proven beyond doubt that, if a more reliable aircraft could be found for Arctic conditions, aerial exploration was the answer.

Wilkins bought two small Stinson biplanes for a series

of flights involving landings on the polar ice away from base. The single-engined aircraft had a specially covered-in cockpit area. With Eielson as pilot he took off on a 1000-kilometre flight towards the Pole to search for unknown islands. They were within 80 kilometres of their turn-around point when the engine began to miss and they were forced to land on the ice pack. Wilkins and Eielson were able to fix the fault and carried on. Airborne again, they ran into severe storms and soon realised that they would not have sufficient fuel to return to base. They were still 160 kilometres short of Point Barrow when the tanks ran dry and they landed on the ice in near total darkness.

It was then that Wilkins' years with Stefansson and the Eskimos were to pay off. Within hours he had built a snow igloo and then moved in the rations and survival gear that the explorer had always insisted be stowed in the aircraft. That night, as the storm blew itself out, they sat snug and warm feasting on pemmican, biscuits, raisins and hot chocolate.

Next morning Wilkins built a makeshift sled out of air-craft parts and, with 32-kilogram packs on their backs, they commenced the long trek home. The men took turns in pulling the loaded sled across the frozen Arctic sea ice. It was no easy task. One was harnessed to the front of the sled while the other helped guide it over and around the crevasses and shelves formed by the ever-shifting ice pack. Wilkins was alarmed to discover that his companion was suffering from severe frostbite. Eielson had frozen his right hand while working on the cantankerous engine that had forced them down. His fingers were turning black and the hand was useless.

Day after day they inched their way towards the settle-ment. Wilkins carefully plotted the course with a pocket compass and two watches. They were crossing a fairly open sheet of sea ice when Eielson heard the terrifying sound of cracking ice. He turned just in time to see his companion disappear through a hole in the ice into the freezing Arctic Sea. Unable to help, he stood transfixed. Wilkins' head was still above water and he yelled at the young American to spread-eagle himself on the ice to prevent any further cracking. With a superhuman effort Wilkins released his heavy pack and threw it up alongside his companion. Then somehow he managed to struggle back from certain death on to the ice.

In the sub-zero temperature the Australian knew he would freeze to death within minutes if he did not get out of his wet clothes. He did the only thing possible and stripped to the skin, then capered about in the relatively warm snow to restore circulation. Luckily he had spare snow boots and underclothes for within seconds his discarded clothes were frozen solid. They lay stiff on the ice like parts of some strange dismembered scarecrow. By rubbing his deerskin and fur outer garments with snow he was able to make them sufficiently soft and dry to wear again.

The nightmare journey ended thirteen days later when, given up for dead, they walked back to the settlement.

Wilkins returned to the United States determined to find a more reliable aircraft before he undertook the long transpolar flight. While there, he met another Australian flyer looking for an aircraft. Charles Kingsford Smith was making plans for his trans-Pacific crossing. Wilkins struck a bargain with Smithy, selling him his three-motored Fokker *Detroiter*.

The aircraft was in fact a hybrid, for it was supposedly built from parts of both of Wilkins' damaged Fokkers. An American journalist wrote later: "In the glow of the midnight sun, with a mass of wreckage as the father, with necessity as the mother, and Sir Hubert as the midwife, the *Southern Cross* was born."

With the coming of summer, the exploration team returned to Point Barrow, where two new Lockheed Vega monoplanes were transported. Renowned for their sleek lines and reliability, they were considered the best aircraft for the job. Even by today's standards, the Vega was a beautiful aircraft.

Following a thorough cold weather workout, Wilkins and Eielson commenced their preparations for the big trip. Into the Lockheed's capacious fuselage they stowed survival gear and food light in weight but high in nutrition: pemmican, biscuits, raisins, malted milk, chocolate. Rifles, small tents, snowshoes, a primus stove and spare engine oil were among the gear they might need to survive the transpolar crossing.

The route to Spitzbergen, their destination on the other side of the top of the world, would be a navigator's nightmare. No landmarks on the barren ice would help plot their course over the ice cap. Magnetic compasses are virtually useless in the area of the Pole and are subject to huge variation errors, so Sir Hubert was faced with relying mainly on the use of sextant and chronometer to fix position by the sun — providing, of course, the sun co-operated and was not obscured by polar storms.

On 3 April 1928 the weather was clear and the Eskimos had prepared a strip in the snow 3500 feet long. At 3 a.m. the long engine start-up procedure commenced. Heating stoves were lit under the covers to protect the engine from the bitter cold. Wilkins placed cans of engine oil on primus stoves and slowly heated them to near boiling point. An hour later the steaming oil was poured into the now-hot motor. The pilot climbed aboard and, scraping the ice off his windscreen, peered down while the navigator prepared to swing the propeller.

This was a critical time. If they were unable to start within a few minutes, the engine would become too cold in the minus 6^{0}C wind. "Switches off?" "Switches off," Eielson replied. "Gas on?" "Gas on," came the affirmative. "All clear?" "All clear." On the first swing the plane coughed, crackled and then broke into a steady purr. They were ready.

Wilkins climbed aboard into his rear cockpit area and

willing helpers gave the Vega a helping push to break the
snow's freezing hold on the skis. They watched as the aircraft roared down the strip, blowing great plumes of dry
snow behind it. Their cheers turned to silent alarm as the
aircraft failed to lift. The pilot cut the engine as the Vega
approached the great snow bank at the end of the run, and
the plane ground to a stop amid a great cloud of snow.

To everyone's relief, the aircraft received only minor
damage to its skis, but it was impossible to leave that day.
The runway was far too short for the heavily loaded aircraft. For a week they toiled, carving a longer take-off run
out of the great snow banks. Two more take-off attempts
failed. After each they lengthened the strip further.

The dawn was clear and still on 16 April. The strip now
measured close to a mile, and the long start-up procedure
was commenced again. The engine burst into life on the
first swing. With a push from the groundcrew, the Vega
quickly gathered speed. At 130 kph Eielson eased back on
the control column and they were airborne.

They climbed steadily to 500 feet and set heading. After
two hours Wilkins wrote in the log "Engine Revs 1725.
Engine Temp 120. First leg Groundspeed 108 mph 10 left
drift." Everything was going well.

During the early hours of the flight, their only problem
was the intense cold, for the Lockheed had no cabin heating system and the temperature inside was minus 2^0C.
They were thankful for Wilkins' insistence that they wear
Eskimo-type clothing in the aircraft. Over wool and silk
underclothes they wore shirts and pants of oiled deerskin
and outer garments of fur.

At the low level they could pick out in detail the ice
pack, the huge crevasses and ridges continually formed
and unformed by the moving ice. The movement was once
so turbulent that great lumps of ice were thrown into the
air with an audible explosion. Wilkins remembered when
he had crossed the ice on foot with the dream of travelling
above it just as he was now.

They were eleven hours out of Point Barrow when they ran into an Arctic storm. It was so cold that the engine temperature dropped to a dangerously low 15^{0}C; if it could not be raised they were in trouble. Eielson solved the problem by opening the throttle and climbing slowly. It was past midnight but the never-setting summer sun still hovered on the horizon. As the storm worsened and huge cloud banks barred their path, they decided it would be suicidal to continue. Selecting a clear area on the ice they landed to weather out the storm. So strong was the headwind that the aircraft stopped within 10 metres of touchdown.

They secured the aircraft against the wind and quickly drained the engine oil. (Otherwise it would freeze solid within fifteen minutes.) The engine covered, the two men settled down in the aircraft to eat their first meal. Wilkins had managed to get a final sun shot before they hit the storm and estimated they were down somewhere on Grants Land. All night the aircraft shook and shuddered in the violent storm. Early next day the wind dropped and the sun reappeared. They headed on, but were now picking up headwind along the route, and were concerned to find their fuel consumption higher than expected.

Twenty hours' flying time out from Point Barrow, they sighted the mountains of Spitzbergen. But their relief was short-lived, for heading towards them was the most violent storm either man had ever seen. The area where they knew their destination at Green Harbour lay was covered with towering clouds. Again they must land and weather the storm. They came down in an area known as Dead Man's Island, not a particularly cheerful thought, and battened down just before the storm broke on them, it lasted for five long days!

When the wind had abated sufficiently, it was necessary to check the fuel. With habitation about one flying hour away, at their present rate of consumption they needed 56 litres of petrol. The cabin tanks had been used earlier, so they drained the two wing tanks. As the last drop ran out they had measured a mere 38 litres. It was not enough. Wilkins decided to cut into the lowest part of the auxiliary cabin tanks to drain any unused dregs. If they were lucky, a few litres might be produced from each. And each few litres meant a couple of miles less on foot if they came down short of their destination. To their delight, an extra 18 litres came rushing out of each tank. With 74 litres of fuel, they had sufficient to make it, plus about fifteen minutes to spare. They quickly prepared the aircraft for their final leg.

There was an area of about 100 feet in front of the Vega that they had trampled over and over again to form a hard surface. This should be enough to gather speed on before completing the take-off run on soft snow. The only problem was to loosen the skis from the frozen hold of the snow. With both men on board and full power, the aircraft would not budge. Wilkins would have to get out and start the plane moving.

It seemed simple, but it wasn't. The next thirty minutes were to be the most terrifying of his life. The Australian trailed a rope ladder out of the rear hatch and climbed down on to the snow. With the engine at full power, he leant with all his weight on the rear of the aircraft. Suddenly it came unstuck and gathered speed. Blinded by snow and slipstream from the propeller he was unable to climb up to the hatch on top of the fuselage. Exhausted he fell back into the snow as the aircraft gathered speed. Unable to see to the rear, Eielson was unaware that his navigator was not on board He took off and only when he circled the area did he realise what had happened. He quickly landed.

For the second attempted take-off, Wilkins planned to grab the rope ladder as soon as the Lockheed started to move. This was how Wilkins described the ordeal:

We started up again and as the machine gathered speed I tried to climb to the tail and from there struggled desperately to gain the cockpit. I had thrown off my mittens to get a good grip on the rope ladder. My hands were soon numbed with the cold and I could not readily grip the rope, so I grabbed hold with my teeth.

A foolish thing to do perhaps but it seemed imperative that I cling somehow to the machine. We had gathered speed and Eielson, feeling the weight still on the tail, thought I was safe and took off. Just before leaving the ground I realised that my chances of gaining the cockpit in the air were much too small and I let go and slithered from the smooth shiny fuselage, was struck by the tail and thrown into a snowdrift. Fortunately it was soft.

Fortunate indeed, for at that time the Vega would have accelerated to close on 130 kph. Eielson circled and landed again. He found his companion stunned but, amazingly, uninjured . . . that is unless you counted a full set of loose front teeth!

Now in a critical situation, they judged there was only sufficient fuel left for one more take-off and the flight to Green Harbour. If Wilkins could not get on board the next time, the American would have to leave him behind. They off-loaded a tent and supplies as precautions.

For their final attempt, Wilkins hooked one leg inside the hatch and with the other dangling overboard, threw all his weight against the fuselage while straining against a piece of wood. They had also lifted the tail to a flying position on a cairn built of snow blocks. For a few agonising moments the aircraft refused to move as the pilot jammed the rudders to free the skis by a sideways motion. Wilkins saw the skis "fishtailing" and pushing the offending snow to the side; suddenly the Vega leapt forward. He was thrown through the hatch and lay huddled exhausted but ecstatic on the cabin floor.

Thirty minutes later they sighted the tall radio masts of Green Harbour.

On his return to England, Hubert Wilkins was knighted by King George V and presented with the Royal Geographical Society's Patron's Medal "for his many years of systematic work in the polar regions, culminating in his remarkable flight from Point Barrow to Spitzbergen''.

Sir Hubert continued with his polar research. Again accompanied by his close friend Eielson, he took the two Vegas to Antarctica and made several important pioneering flights. In 1929, he married a beautiful Australian actress named Suzanne Bennett.

Still hankering to get back to the Arctic, he purchased a surplus United States Navy submarine for the token sum of one dollar. He named her the *Nautilus* and planned to sail her beneath the polar ice cap. However, after making several trial dives beneath the ice, he abandoned the scheme. His dream was made a reality by an American nuclear submarine following the Second World War.

On yet another trip to the Land of the Midnight Sun, Wilkins mounted a gigantic search for a lost Russian aircraft. With a crew of four, Levanevsky (the Russian Lindbergh) took off to fly to the North Pole, and was never seen again. A radio distress call was picked up saying they were landing on the ice. Several weak calls were received much later. In the search, Wilkins flew over 114 000 square kilometres and searched a total of 460 000 square kilometres, but no trace of the Russians was ever found.

In 1936 Wilkins was involved in yet another epic ''first flight'', this time as a passenger. Since his abortive attempt to mount a transpolar airship flight, he had been fascinated by the thought of travel by lighter-than-air craft.

The German airship *Hindenburg* was to inaugurate the first North Atlantic passenger air service. Accompanied by his wife, Wilkins was one of the few honoured guests amongst a band of journalists and VIPs who boarded the giant airship at Friedrichshafen at 10 a.m. on 6 May 1936. Commanded by its designer, Dr Hugo Eckener, the *Hindenburg* made the maiden crossing to New York in sixty hours.

During the voyage, Lady Wilkins made radio history when she sang to the guests and crew in the ship's lounge, accompanied on the piano by Professor Franz Wagner. Broadcast by the *Hindenburg's* radio to New York from over mid-Atlantic by the "flying announcer" Dr Max Jordan, this concert was then relayed from station WJZ over the NBC network across the United States.

Sir Hubert spent many hours in the command gondola with the crew, fascinated by the precise and skilful operation of the monster airship. However, he had some misgivings about the large black swastikas painted on its tail. Following the *Hindenburg's* triumphal passage over Manhattan Island and Times Square, it moored at the nearby Lakehurst Naval Station. It was at Lakehurst, one year to the day from the start of her maiden voyage, that the *Hindenburg* caught fire and crashed whilst mooring, with the loss of thirty-six lives.

In his later years, Sir Hubert Wilkins was appointed Polar Adviser to the United States government and settled in America, but never ceased to call himself an Australian. In all, Sir Hubert Wilkins made thirty expeditions to the polar regions. He never retired and on the day of his death was working on his car only a few moments before he died.

It is hard to understand how any man would happily devote a lifetime to wandering the frozen ends of the world. They are places of incredible hardship entailing a ceaseless battle merely to survive. Even Sir Hubert Wilkins was at a loss to explain: "People often ask me why I go to the polar regions. I doubt if any one of us can say in so many words just why we do this, that or the other. I might fill volumes telling why I go to the Arctic or Antarctic, yet the man who doesn't 'know' would still not understand."

9
The Quiet Hero

A thick grey mist hung over London's Croydon Airport at dawn on 7 February 1928, and clung to the silver fabric of the tiny Avro Avian biplane. Just four people stood quietly watching as a stocky man in a double-breasted lounge suit climbed aboard, started the engine and took off. Within moments he had disappeared into the early morning fog, and into history.

Of the dawn quartet, one was the pilot's wife and one worked for the aircraft's manufacturer. The others were total strangers, casual passers-by on an early morning stroll.

The pilot, Bert Hinkler, was on his way home to Australia and was to receive recognition as one of the greatest solo long-distance flyers of all time. When he arrived in Australia fifteen and a half days, 17 500 kilometres and nineteen stops later, millions around the world were talking about "Hustling Hinkler"! They recognised the challenge of man and machine against fatigue, the elements and just sheer distance.

The young Australian had already made one attempt to fly to Australia. In 1920, flying an Avro "Baby", he had reached Turin before his route was blocked by a war in the Middle East.

Since leaving the Naval Air Service after the First World War armistice, Hinkler had been employed as a test pilot by A.V. Roe Ltd. He had gained a reputation for flying perfection, but his technique was almost fussiness.

This was probably a legacy of his early aviation days in Australia, when he had worked as a mechanic for an American barnstorming pilot, A.B. "Wizard" Stone. As a youth he had built and flown gliders in his home town of Bundaberg, Queensland.

His dream was to fly solo to Australia and demonstrate that aircraft were a safe and cheap method of transportation, not simply the playthings of suicidal fools. He had been unable to find backers. The few who might have been prepared to finance such a "harebrained scheme" wanted a dashing showman, not a quiet, serious young man who shunned publicity. This attitude was to plague Hinkler throughout his career. Yet it sparked his determination to go it alone and lifted him above the level of his contemporaries. True to form, Hinkler had made no announcement of his second attempt to fly to Australia. He was up at 4.30 a.m., having snatched only a couple of hours sleep. He had worked late into the night on last-minute preparations. Although the weather was not ideal, it was too late to delay the flight and the forecast showed improvement over the Mediterranean.

His wife Nancy handed him a small package of sandwiches, biscuits and chocolate which he stowed with a flask of coffee in the Avian's cramped open cockpit. Hinkler shook hands with the manager of the Avro factory, kissed his wife and climbed quickly into G-EBOV's cockpit. Placed carefully beside his seat was a copy of the *Times* world atlas, the only publication he could find with maps covering the whole of his route to Darwin.

The aircraft's 85-horsepower Cirrus engine was at full revs as the heavily fuel-laden biplane clawed its way up and out over London. The pilot snuggled down beneath the upturned collar of the overcoat worn against the chill of the English winter, and set heading for the English Channel. Within minutes the lights of the city disappeared into the darkness of the early morning and he was forced to fly on the Avian's few basic instruments.

The weather did not improve until Hinkler had crossed France and was approaching the Swiss Alps, when a break in the overcast allowed him to fix his position. Until then it had been "dead reckoning", which meant flying an accurate compass course. The Avian cruised at around 120 kph, a speed comparable with that of a modern family car. Hinkler had climbed to 8000 feet over the mountains and it was bitterly cold. His lounge suit, overcoat, flying helmet and goggles were not the ideal outfit for such conditions.

He crossed the Alps in daylight, but by the time he reached Rome for the first landing, night had fallen and low clouds obscured the ground. He circled above the clouds looking vainly for a break and signalling with a pocket torch. The moon rose and finally came to his aid, disclosing a break between two huge cloud masses.

He descended and quickly sighted an aerodrome. Minutes later he landed by moonlight — and was immediately arrested. Only when he was being marched to the lock-up between two grim-faced soldiers did Hinkler discover that he had missed Rome's civil airport and landed at a restricted military aerodrome. The airman spent an anxious and fitful four hours on a hard cot before he was rescued by the British consul.

As he walked to his aircraft early next morning, the young Australian was tired and worried. Though he had made good time on the first leg, a fast thirteen hours, he had only managed six hours' rest over the previous two days. Fatigue could be fatal.

Hinkler looked around the airport as he reached the Avian. He felt a shiver run down his spine, for all the approaches were surrounded by towering radio masts. The previous night he must have flown right between them on his landing approach! That he could have missed colliding with one seemed an impossibility; no wonder the Italian authorities had been so concerned.

Leaving Rome, he crossed the Italian countryside. In clear conditions he was able to look down into the smoking crater of Mt Vesuvius and the rock face of Mt Etna. Over the turquoise blue water of the Mediterranean, the Cirrus motor droned on. It did not miss a beat and his landing at Malta was ahead of schedule.

Hinkler was given a noisy reception by the Royal Air Force detachment stationed on the tiny island. It was late when he finally managed to drag himself away and get his first good night's sleep.

The following day he crossed into North Africa, refuelled at Benghazi, and headed for Tobruk. He missed his target by 60 kilometres and was forced to make a desert landing amongst dense camel thorn. The Avian was undamaged and Hinkler decided to spend the night beneath the wing. He inflated his rubber dinghy and settled down to sleep.

Next morning a group of Arabs cleared a path through the stunted thorn bushes for Hinkler's take-off. The airman was fortunate to come across the Arabs and even luckier that they were friendly. Many of the early flyers were attacked by the wandering tribesmen of the desert. An hour later he was refuelling at Tobruk.

Following another night under the wing at the Palestine border, the lone airman flew on to the Royal Air Force base at Jaffa. After the bitter cold of Europe, he was now facing a new problem with the excessive heat over the Middle East causing agonising bouts of cramp. He also suffered periods of depression and resorted to singing and talking to himself to overcome their effect.

At Jaffa the RAF checked the Avian thoroughly and declared it in perfect condition. Then they took him to the Officers' Mess for a celebration. Next morning he was delayed when caught up in a diphtheria scare. Medical clearances, customs and bureaucratic red tape whittled the day away and Hinkler was forced to spend a second night with his generous hosts.

Early next morning he was off again on the 1600-kilometre flight to Basra. During the nine-and-a-half-hour flight he was again hit by violent leg cramps and periods of depression. When he finally arrived at Basra, the airport was deserted. Only after he had spent several hours servicing the engine did the curious observers turn up to watch their unexpected visitor. It was past midnight when he finished.

Over Arabia, Hinkler was already five days ahead of the time set by the Smith brothers in 1919. The world press, who up to that time had ignored the flight, were suddenly starting to show interest. It was obvious that if he could maintain the pace, the Australian would set a new record to India. However, they were still sceptical. "He can't keep it up," the pundits wrote. They explained that long flights in little aircraft generally ended in failure.

The leg between Jask, on the Gulf of Oman, and Karachi almost proved the "experts" right. Soon after take-off, Hinkler saw with dismay that fuel was slowly leaking from the tank located in the centre section of the upper wing. For seven nerve-racking hours he flew on, his eyes constantly moving between his fuel gauge, his watch and his airspeed indicator.

Luck was with him and he raced the fuel leak to a safe landing at Karachi's Royal Air Force landing ground. By 1 a.m. he had completed the repairs himself. Two and a half hours later he was on his way again . . . now holding the record for the fastest flight to India.

The world press were suddenly waxing lyrical over the flight. One staid and conservative British newspaper coined the phrase "Hustling Hinkler" which was taken up all around the world and stuck for the rest of the airman's life. An American composer picked up the theme and while Hinkler was still winging his way to Australia, Tin Pan Alley pianists were playing the latest sheet music hit, "Hustling Hinkler up in the Sky". But still the doubt lingered: "Can he keep it up?"

Across India the tiring airman battled heat, dust storms and a severe headache. He had taken well-meaning advice at Karachi and discarded his flying helmet in favour of a tropical pith helmet as protection against the fierce sun. But his ears had lost the protection afforded by a flying helmet against the roar of wind and motor.

On 17 February he left Calcutta and headed for Rangoon. Smoke from vast jungle fires over Burma cut visibility to zero. He later wrote that the fires "covered the ground like the matted hair of a Fijian". Approaching Rangoon, the Avian battled its way through huge tropical storms. They were a foretaste of the deadly intertropical storm front that still lay between him and Australia.

En route to Singapore he was forced 100 kilometres off course by a murderous storm and made an emergency landing in a jungle clearing.

He eventually arrived at Singapore only to be admonished by airport officials for not having landed at the local racecourse! It was just as well, for tropical rainstorms had waterlogged the track. As it was, when he attempted to get airborne at the aerodrome next morning, his heavily laden biplane bogged in the rain-sodden grass. It took a massive push from enthusiastic onlookers to get the Avro moving. He staggered into the air bound for Java.

Over Batavia Hinkler had to circle for two hours awaiting a break in the storm clouds of the intertropical front.

On the fourteenth day, battered by tropical storms, he reached Bima, the jumping-off place for the dreaded crossing of the lonely Timor Sea to Darwin. Up before dawn, he ate two bananas for breakfast, since it was too early to get a proper meal. In the early morning half-light, loaded to the gills with fuel, the Avro climbed slowly out over the mountains and headed for Australia. A daunting 1360 kilometres of shark-infested ocean lay between Hinkler and the record.

Crowds had been gathering all day at Darwin's Fanny Bay Aerodrome. By late afternoon many were wondering if their gallant Australian airman was down. It seemed he was long overdue. Some were preparing to leave when a man with a telescope let out a cry. There at a terrific height over Darwin was a tiny black insect buzzing down between the clouds. As it came lower and circled the crowd, it became a silver aeroplane. Soon they could read the letters G-EBOV on the fuselage. Hinkler was home!

As the aircraft came to a standstill, the crowd went mad. They surged forward to watch the small, unshaven, sunburnt man, in a dirty crumpled double-breasted suit, climb slowly out of the cockpit. As they roared their approval, he seemed bewildered and embarrassed by the adulation, but finally managed a shy grin.

In fifteen days Bert Hinkler and Avro's amazing Avian had set six major records: first non-stop flight London-Rome; fastest flight England-India; fastest flight England-Australia; first solo flight England-Australia; longest light aircraft flight ever; and the longest solo flight ever made. No wonder Australia lionised its new hero.

In an unprecedented display of national affection, the public took this modest man to their heart. He was the kind of hero with whom they could identify, epitomising the qualities of unobtrusive pride and quiet determination that appealed to a growing new nation.

King George V telegrammed his congratulations and awarded Hinkler the Air Force Cross, the first awarded a civilian pilot. The Commonwealth government made him an honorary Squadron Leader in the RAAF — a title he never used. The public called for him to receive a knighthood. This became a political battle, and most people were convinced it was not awarded because he was a working man's son.

Through it all, Hinkler remained above the ballyhoo. Though ill at ease, he made speeches trying to emphasise the goals of his flight, which were to prove the safety of flying and the role the aircraft had to play in Australia's future. He soon tired of the incessant round of official functions attended by overbearing VIPs and hangers-on. They only saw the hero and bathed in his reflected glory, and were not really interested in what he had set out to prove.

Disillusioned, Hinkler returned to England and formed a small company building the revolutionary "Ibis", a highly successful amphibian of his own design. But the Depression hit and the company failed.

In 1931 Hinkler again hit world headlines with the first west-east solo crossing of the South Atlantic. The flight, made almost continually in cloud, is recognised as an unparalleled navigation feat. Hinkler made landfall just 16 kilometres from his destination.

Hinkler was killed in 1933, when he crashed in the Italian Alps attempting to better C.W.A. Scott's record of eight and a half days between England and Australia. His death heralded the end of an aviation era. The lone pioneer was soon to be replaced, as flying entered an age of increasing sophistication. With it came cabin multi-engined aircraft, radio and radio navigation equipment with specialist crew members. There were still routes to pioneer, but somehow they lost a little of the glamour of the long-distance flyer taking on the seemingly impossible.

Amongst that select band of pioneers, Bert Hinkler in his Avro Avian reigned supreme.

10
America Dubbed Her
"the Australian Aviatrix"

Event number 26 was over. A hundred thousand people had watched the Beechcraft Mystery Ship carve up the fastest military aircraft in America to win the Thompson Trophy Speed Race at the 1929 National Air Races in Cleveland, Ohio.

The next event was the 80-kilometre closed-circuit pylon race for women pilots. Favourites with the crowd were Phoebe Omlie and an up-and-coming young woman flyer named Amelia Earhart.

By the end of the first lap the two were ahead of the field but closely followed by an unknown pilot flying a Fleet biplane. The second time around the Fleet had nosed ahead of Amelia Earhart's aircraft and was tailing Phoebe Omlie. Coming into the fifth and last lap, third-placed Amelia Earhart was disqualified for trying to pass the unknown pilot on the inside of the turn — her place had been taken by England's socialite flyer Lady Mary Heath.

In this order they passed the finishing line only seconds apart. Backers of Miss Omlie were congratulating themselves when the crowd hushed for an announcement: "Miss Phoebe Omlie has been disqualified for cutting a corner. The race has been awarded to the second place aircraft, the Fleet biplane flown by Australian woman pilot Mrs Keith Miller."

Thus for the second time Jessie "Chubbie" Miller, wife of a Melbourne journalist, had made aviation headlines. But this time as a pilot in her own right. Her first record flight had been as a passenger-cum-assistant pilot to British long-distance flyer Captain Bill Lancaster. Technically she had been the first passenger to make a flight from England to Australia.

It seems that only her passenger flight has been remembered in her native land. Probably because the brief years that her aviation star glowed were in American skies. It is surprising that Chubbie Miller is not listed among Australia's early flyers. In America she was known as "the Australian aviatrix".

Born of an English clergyman's son and an Australian clergyman's daughter, Chubbie had a sheltered and restricted upbringing. At the age of 18 she married journalist Keith Miller, only five years her senior. She was naive and unsophisticated; he, raw and immature. Temperamentally unsuited and with little in common, they quickly grew apart. They tried hard to keep the marriage together, but a few years later Chubbie was alone in England – allegedly on a six-month holiday.

There she met English airman Bill Lancaster, who was desperately trying to find backers for a planned flight to Australia. It was to be the first by a light aircraft but, a poor financial organiser, he had met with little success. He too was married but living apart. Chubbie persuaded Lancaster to agree to take her along if she could raise half the cash needed. She eventually raised most of the money. Her forthrightness, candour and surprising business skill won over a score of backers.

On 14 October 1927 the pair took off for Australia in the Avro Avian *Red Rose*. They got to within a day's flight of Darwin when the engine failed on take-off from Muntok Island and *Red Rose* was severely damaged in a forced landing. The aircraft took three months to repair and they were still grounded when Australia's Bert Hinkler passed through on his record-setting flight. Though bitterly disappointed to see the Bundaberg pilot steal their thunder, they generously helped by guarding Hinkler's Avro Avian while the exhausted flyer caught a few hours' sleep.

When the pair eventually reached Australia on 19 March 1928 they were given a great welcome. Though no longer the first civil aircraft to make it, theirs was still the first passenger flight — and a woman passenger at that!

Chubbie had got the flying bug. On the long flight Bill had let her spell him at the controls and she had shown a natural aptitude. Now she must learn to fly properly: not just holding the machine level in the cruise. She must also master take-offs, landings and the other skills necessary to gain a pilot licence.

Lancaster and Chubbie were in love. Once in Australia they continued the partnership. She was much in demand to lecture on their flight. A lecture-tour contract at a fee of £150 a week took them all over the country and Lancaster flew Chubbie from town to town.

A chance meeting in Brisbane started a long chain of events that was to take the pair to America — Chubbie to become a well-known aviation personality; Bill to go on trial for murder and to eventually die of thirst in the Sahara.

While in Brisbane, Lancaster was contracted to fly a photographic mission for the arrival of Kingsford Smith and Ulm in the *Southern Cross* at the end of their epic trans-Pacific flight.

They became close friends with Harry Lyon, the American navigator of the *Southern Cross*. "Mrs Lyon's son, Harry", as the immensely popular navigator introduced himself, showed the pair a cable he had received from Hollywood offering $75 000 for Smithy and his crew to help make an aviation film. As Kingsford Smith and Ulm had decided to stay in Australia, Lyons offered Chubbie and Bill their places.

When the three adventurers and the *Southern Cross* radio operator, James Warner, arrived by sea in San Francisco, they were given a ticker tape welcome. It was largely for the two Americans, but the friendly citizens of California included Bill and Chubbie in recognition of their England-Australia flight.

The Hollywood film venture fell through, so the Lyon-Miller-Lancaster partnership decided to make a trans-Atlantic flight. They engaged the Hall Aircraft Company to build a special, long-range aircraft. Chubbie Miller went to Los Angeles to learn Morse code and radio procedures. She was to be co-pilot/radio operator on the flight. Eventually, following numerous delays, the Atlantic flight was scrapped after Hall ran into problems with the machine and its engine.

Lancaster was offered a job as chief test and demonstration pilot for the American Cirrus Engine Company.

Chubbie decided it was time to learn to fly. She enrolled at the Red Bank Aviation School in New Jersey and studied secretly for her pilot's licence. The American press had taken it for granted that she was a licensed pilot on their record flight and it did not seem timely to correct that impression. She gained her licence quickly and easily and in 1929 she was one of only thirty-four women to hold an American licence.

It was time to start putting it to use and earning some money. She heard that the first open Women's Air Race was being organised as part of the National Air Races. The press immediately nicknamed it the "Powder Puff Derby" – a name which has struck to this day. It was an ideal opportunity to make her name.

The route ran from Los Angeles across the continent to Cleveland – a distance of 4300 kilometres. Though she might be inexperienced at handling an aircraft, she well knew the rigours of long-distance flying and Chubbie managed to persuade the Bell Aircraft Corporation to lend her a new Fleet biplane. They completely rebuilt the cockpit around her (at 155 centimetres, she was much smaller than the average male pilot) and she flew the 4000 kilometres to

Los Angeles in easy stages. It was an ideal work-up for the big race.

Hers was one of nineteen aircraft that lined up for the start at Santa Monica on 18 August 1929. The race was to average nearly 600 kilometres a day for eight days. It was timed to reach Cleveland on 26 August when the closed-circuit speed races were planned to start.

Only six of the women made the first checkpoint at Phoenix, Arizona that night – one was Amelia Earhart, another was Chubbie Miller. One of the contestants was out of the race forever. Marvel Crossan had crashed in the desert where, at the last moment, she had tried to parachute from her spinning aircraft, but had been too close to the ground. She was found a short distance from the wreckage where it was seen that her parachute had not opened.

Despite great public pressure to abandon the race, the women were determined to carry on. Amelia Earhart and Chubbie shared a room that night after both had decided that the public would have to get used to the idea of women taking risks in aviation. Women pilots were there to stay. "We all felt terrible but we knew that we had to carry on and finish the race," Amelia Earhart told pressmen on reaching Cleveland.

After a good start, the Australian woman finished well down in the field. She had been up with the leaders when her aircraft ran out of fuel over Arizona. She made a perfect forced landing in desert country where, cursing her primitive and inaccurate fuel gauge, she lost valuable time searching for help and fuel. When she finally got airborne again she was unable to catch the leaders, but Chubbie had the satisfaction of making Cleveland on the assigned day and was third in the light aircraft class.

The Bell Company were delighted that their aircraft had even reached Cleveland within the allotted time and entered Chubbie in the women's closed-circuit speed race. It was this race that pushed her into the headlines. Following her unexpected victory, she entered in two more events, gaining a second and a third place – not a bad performance for a young woman who had only learnt to fly a few months earlier.

With Bill Lancaster in hospital recuperating from a bad aircraft accident in Trinidad, Chubbie decided to reach for the top of the women pilots' totem. She was approached by the Fairchild Aircraft Company. They wanted her to fly one of their latest machines in the 8000-kilometre Ford Reliability Tour. She was one of only three women among the thirty-eight starters. Photographers jostled to snap the Australian girl as she posed by her aircraft. Both she and the machine were in spectacular black and white colours: her white kid jodhpurs, white silk shirt, white jacket and white flying helmet were set off by black boots and tie. The white Fairchild aircraft had a single black line down its fuselage and the results were startling enough to catch the eye of aviation and fashion writers alike.

In this race, Chubbie proved she was not just a show pony. Against the toughest male opposition, she finished eighth overall and was the only woman to complete the race. Suddenly she was not just famous with the huge crowds who followed the aviation circuit and who tended to rank women pilots only in respect of their performance against other women but, more importantly, she was now judged by her aviation peers in respect of her performance as a pilot rather than as a woman who flew aeroplanes. There was quite a difference – particularly with so many women taking to the air just to be fashionable. The men of aviation did not generally take them too seriously, but there were exceptions. Chubbie Miller had joined that elite band. Fairchilds doubled her prizemoney and sponsoring companies sent fat cheques. At last the money was pouring in.

Her flying career seemed assured and Mrs Keith Miller – as she was known in America – was much in demand. But late in 1929 her good fortune nosedived with the great stock market crash. The booming aviation business slowed, stopped and then fell apart. Lancaster's latest job with the Victor Aircraft Company dissolved when that company went into receivership. Chubbie was unable to find work and bills started mounting.

For a few months in 1930 they both worked as demonstration and sales pilots for the Stork Corporation until it, too, faced bankruptcy. Out of work again, Chubbie realised that the only way to make money from flying was to attempt record-breaking or trail-blazing flights. She decided to try a 10 000-kilometre flight to Japan – no one had yet made the flight.

She approached the Wright Engine Company which agreed to lend her an engine. But they categorically refused her permission to use it on the long, overwater flight to Japan. It is obvious that the Wright Company considered that the flight had little chance of success and would gain only bad publicity if she went missing. Instead they suggested that she set a new coast-to-coast record and, reluctantly, she agreed. The loan of a new Whirlwind engine was too good to miss.

Her search for a suitable airframe for the flight ended at the factory of the Denver-based Alexander Company. They had a low-wing monoplane called the Alexander Bullet gathering dust in a hangar. The Bullet had never been granted a certificate of airworthiness. During test flights the model had been found hard to control and to have vicious spinning tendencies. The first company test pilot had resigned after preliminary test flights. He refused to continue, stating that the aircraft was unsafe. The second test pilot had baled out after another prototype had entered an irrecoverable spin. A specialist in testing stalls and spin manoeuvres was then employed. His aircraft spun straight into the ground. The unfortunate pilot baled out but too late – his parachute had only half opened when he hit the ground. He later died of terrible injuries.

The remaining prototype was put into storage. This was

the "killer" aircraft that Chubbie begged to use. The company wanted no part of her offer (the aircraft was not even certificated, they told her) and only after she explained that she had no wish to do any stunt flying and wanted only to fly straight and level from coast to coast did they agree.

They installed her Wright Whirlwind engine, repainted the airframe and gave the machine a thorough overhaul. Then, to her surprise, they gave her the machine for nothing. It is possible that Don Alexander, the president of Alexander Industries, a company which was also well established as makers of motion-picture commercials, saw little to lose in giving the Australian woman the unsuccessful aircraft. If she set a record, Alexander could cash in on the good publicity to help re-establish the aviation division's rather tarnished name. If, however, she crashed it could do little more to damage the already dreadful reputation of the Bullet. He would merely have to suggest that Chubbie had not flown in accordance with her plans and the company's advice to operate well away from speeds and situations likely to cause a spin.

While Chubbie was making her final plans, news arrived that another woman, Laura Ingalls, was already in the air attempting to beat the record. The American made New York to Los Angeles in just over thirty hours' flight time — a new record. The press went wild and Laura Ingalls was headline news.

Rather than detract from Chubbie's plans, this was good news. If she took off straight away and could beat the new record, she would cash in on the publicity already generated by her American opponent.

She left New York on 12 October. The Bullet, with its new 165-horsepower engine, gave no trouble. Equipped with a recent innovation — a retractable undercarriage — the monopolane cruised at 200 kph.

She had to contend with bad weather over the Allegheny Mountains and across the great Midwest and she was thankful to be protected by the enclosed four-seat cabin. It was a vastly different proposition from the open cockpits of the Avro Avian and Fleet biplane where she had been at the mercy of wind and rain.

For hour after hour she battled the weather, wind and fatigue. A major worry in bad weather would have been to ensure that she did not allow herself to get lax at the controls and let her airspeed decay to a point where she might stall and spin. She would have realised that one spin was all she would ever make in the Bullet − it would be fatal.

She made five refuelling stops along the route and at three of them she caught a few hours' sleep. Three days after leaving the east coast she sighted the Pacific ahead − a shimmering backdrop to the Californian desert and the coastal ranges. When she touched down in Los Angeles she had cut Laura Ingalls' record by four hours and forty-three minutes.

Local newspapers carried headlines applauding "Mrs Keith Miller". Leading pilots in America were receiving public adulation similar in many ways to that given to the movie stars. On the west coast in particular, with the recent arrival of talking movies and the crazy Hollywood boom, the press and radio seemed to devote all its attention to "stars", whether they be from films, sport or the exciting new craze of aviation.

The public loved it. In Hollywood, in particular, everyone was a frustrated film star. Waitresses, usherettes, shop assistants, hat check girls − everywhere it seemed budding starlets waited to be discovered. Men in their thousands lined up at the great studios for crowd-scene jobs, hoping for a few seconds on screen that might catch some director's eye.

Flying films were big at the box office. Since the success of *Wings* in 1928, producers had realised aviation films, though expensive to make, rarely failed. They employed hordes of barnstorming pilots for the flying sequences. The fatality rate was alarming, but no one seemed to care as long as the cameras kept turning throughout the unscheduled fatal crashes.

When Chubbie Miller arrived in Los Angeles, Howard Hughes was just finishing his greatest aviation epic *Dawn Patrol*. Had she remained long in Hollywood's dream factory, she might well have joined the long list of pilots making a living flying for the camera. But it was not to be.

Shortly after landing she heard that Laura Ingalls was already trying to go one better than her Australian opponent. The American had taken off on a return west-east record-breaking attempt. Two days later, Chubbie left the bright lights. Taking up the challenge, she headed back to New York and, with the aid of the prevailing intercontinental tailwinds, she made the eastern capital in twenty-one hours and forty-seven minutes, knocking three hours and eight minutes off her American rival's time.

There was no doubt who was champion: she held the transcontinental record both ways. For a while the money rolled in again — newspaper editors and advertisers were prepared to pay big money for articles on her exploits and to use her face and name to promote all sorts of products.

A month later a businessman offered her $1000 and all expenses paid for a flight from Pittsburgh to Havana and return. She was to carry a letter of friendship from the Mayor of Pittsburgh to the President of Cuba.

She planned to make one refuelling stop in Miami during the 2100-kilometre flight, but strong headwinds forced her to make an unscheduled landing at Charleston, where she took on extra fuel and stayed the night. The following afternoon she reached Cuba and was given a hero's welcome. She planned to relax for a few days and make a leisurely return flight, but next morning her sponsor, Harvard R. Smith of Aerial Enterprises Inc., cabled that she was to return as soon as possible.

For the following five days she was grounded by foul weather. Not only was Havana's weather bad, but the forecast along her route to Miami showed poor visibility and very strong winds. She might have delayed longer, but Smith cabled her daily, warning that the company was losing publicity by her delay.

Finally, on 28 November she allowed his pressure to override her better judgment and with only a marginal improvement in the weather she took off on the three-hour direct flight for Miami. In view of the winds, she had taken on fuel for nine hours. Completely confident in her ability to reach the Florida coast, even allowing for strong cross winds and poor visibility, she had refused an offer to fly in formation with the Miami-bound Pan-American airliner. It would have meant another day's wait.

The Bullet no longer worried her. She was completely at home in the aircraft. It was not, however, equipped with instruments to allow flight in cloud, nor was it radio equipped. The circumstances that have to this day spelt disaster to the unwary pilot were evident as Chubbie Miller flew low over the Cuban coast and headed in the direction of Miami: poor weather, no blind-flying instruments, pilot untrained in cloud flying, no radio and worrying business pressure.

A pilot approaching Cuba saw her aircraft low over the sea thirty minutes after the Australian had taken off, then she just disappeared. With her aircraft overdue in Miami, an air search was mounted and six planes took off to search down her track — two more left Havana to search the Cuban end. By dark they had returned with no sign of the missing aircraft.

The search resumed next day without success. The *New York Times* reported: "As nightfall obscured the waters of the Florida Straits hope for the safety of Mrs J.M. Keith Miller, Australian aviatrix, faded until searchers conceded her no more than a thousand-to-one chance of a safe landing."

By the second night the search was called off and aviation officials were reported to believe she had perished attempting the flight in adverse weather conditions.

Only two people pressed for a continued search. One was fellow airwoman Laura Ingalls, who felt sure that Chubbie could well have force-landed safely on an isolated reef or uninhabited part of the Florida coastline. And, of course, Bill Lancaster refused to believe she was dead. He finally persuaded the Navy to lend him an aircraft and he took off from Washington, heading for the search area.

Shortly after Chubbie had left Havana, two days earlier, she had found the winds much stronger than expected. Levelling off at 750 feet to stay out of the solid overcast, she flew her course for an hour. Terrific turbulence had thrown her about the cockpit and she was bruised and shaken. The Bullet, though battered, was riding the weather well and the engine was purring smoothly.

After about two hours she should have seen the islands of the Florida Keys, but they did not appear; instead she was confronted by a solid line of squall clouds. She had no option but to push on through and hope to break out on the other side. She had not planned on the terrific updraughts in the storm and within minutes she was pulled up into the core of the storm. Her compass became useless as it toppled and spun around and she no longer knew in which direction she was heading. Her height became little more than a guess as currents tossed the Bullet up and down. Terrified of losing control and entering a spin, she desperately looked for a break. She had only a primitive "needle and ball" − turn and bank indictor − and the "seat of her pants" to tell her aircraft's altitude. She knew enough not to rely on the latter. Vertigo − incorrect sensing of one's altitude − was the number-one killer of untrained cloud flyers.

Her only chance lay with regaining some visual reference, so she lowered the aircraft's nose and headed down for the water. If the cloud and rain was right on to the surface she was dead, but if there was even a small break below the base she might have a chance.

She broke out of cloud a heart-stopping 60 feet above

the storm-tossed sea, but still there was no sign of land. With her compass still spinning, and no sun for a rough check, she had no idea of the direction in which she was heading. She could be flying into the vast Gulf of Mexico or out into the Atlantic. Totally disorientated, she began to panic.

For another four hours she wandered the sky – once she thought she had found land when the sea turned a light green, but no land came up. She eventually flew out of the storm over a calm and empty sea. Her fuel was getting low and she switched to her reserve tanks – enough for about two more hours.

Sure that she was west of Florida in the Gulf of Mexico, she headed in a rough easterly direction and an hour later she sighted two tiny fishing boats. Should she ditch alongside them? As she circled low, the fishermen pointed excitedly towards the east. She thought that must be the direction of Florida so she decided to carry on for a while.

Within minute she sighted a long, desolate coastline. She turned south for where she believed Miami would be located, but no towns came in sight – only unbroken jungle. After some time she sighted a small village and nearby a small clearing. Mentally and physically exhausted, and concerned with the low fuel state, she decided to attempt a landing. It would be touch and go, but for once the strong winds came to her aid. Combined with the thick undergrowth, they brought the Bullet to a stop well short of the dense jungle on the far end of her landing run. Apart from some torn fabric, the aircraft was undamaged.

She was approached by a group of natives from the village. To her surprise, they addressed her in English and she asked where she was. "Andros Island. We belong to King George," they replied.

No wonder she had not found Florida – she had been blown out into the Atlantic! When she had headed east she was going further away from the American mainland. Had she not hit the island (one of the Bahama group) she would have flown out into the vast Atlantic. Then, when her fuel gave out – probably after another hour – she would have disappeared without trace.

When the news that she was safe reached Bill Lancaster he was mounting his own search in a small seaplane. He flew immediately to the Bahamas. A few days later, the Bullet was airborne again and the pair returned to Miami.

Telegrams flooded in. The news made world headlines. Among the cables congratulating Chubbie on her safe return was one offering her $1500 for the story of her flight. She accepted it.

Cynical elements of the press, caught before perhaps by some way-out publicity stunt, hinted that the whole affair had been a put-up job. There were hectic scenes and tempers flared at a press conference called by Bill Lancaster. Eventually America's leading columnist Walter Winchell joined the controversy, throwing his weight behind the Australian woman. "The ground marks reveal that it was a forced landing and her gas tanks were dry," he wrote. In his opinion, Mrs Miller was honest and sincere.

Still determined to complete the flight and earn the $1000 promised by Harvard Smith, she took off for Pittsburgh a few days later. She had refuelled at Jacksonville and was just airborne on the final leg when the Wright Whirlwind engine stopped without warning. She crashed heavily trying to avoid a line of trees, and though she was unhurt, the Bullet was a virtual write-off.

Harvard R. Smith – businessman to the core – did not pay her the cash award, insisting that she had not fully completed the flight back to Pittsburgh. Aviation was a tough game and such promoters did not help improve the "wheeler dealer" image that surrounded many of the early commercial flying ventures.

Chubbie Miller returned the amazingly undamaged engine to the Wright Company. It was found to have stopped due to a fault in the fuel system. The wreck of the Alexander "Bullet" was later purchased by two flying enthusiasts who eventually rebuilt the monoplane. It did nothing to enhance the aircraft's reputation, for they both lost their lives in it.

The crash of the Bullet was the end of aviation stardom for Chubbie. Though entered in the 1931 Miami All-American Air Meet, she was unable to find an aircraft to contest the speed races. For the remainder of that year she went on a lecture tour of the United States, flying herself from town to town. A proposed transcontinental flight fell through when she developed appendicitis.

In 1932 she and Lancaster headed again for Miami to enter the air races but the aircraft they were to fly never turned up. They decided to stay in Miami and Lancaster got a job with a shady organisation which called itself Latin-American Airways.

Chubbie stayed in Miami to produce a book on her life for a New York publisher for which the pair employed a ghost writer named Hayden Clarke. However, some months later she was in the headlines again: Clarke had been shot and Lancaster arrested for the murder. It seemed that she and Clarke had fallen in love and Lancaster had killed the young writer in a fit of jealousy.

It was late 1932 before Lancaster was acquitted, following a long and sensational court action. The pair, seemingly friendless and broke, left for England in October. Once settled in England, they separated for a time. Chubbie had finally divorced her husband a year earlier, but Lancaster, though separated, still had an English wife.

She took a break from flying, having been offered a substantial sum to serialise her life for a leading British newspaper.

Lancaster bought an Avro Avian, formerly owned by Sir Charles Kingsford Smith, and attempted to set a new record for a flight to Cape Town. He disappeared over the the Sahara and was never seen alive again. Chubbie tried desperately to borrow an aircraft and search for him, but was unable to find a suitable aircraft quickly. She gave up when it had finally become obvious that the airman could no longer be alive.

Chubbie Miller faded from sight and eventually married an airline pilot, but twenty-nine years after Bill Lancaster went missing she was back in the news again. In 1962 a French army patrol found the wreck of Lancaster's *Southern Cross Minor* in an area of the desert known as the Land of Thirst. His mummified body and a diary were near by. He had lived for a week before dying of thirst.

The diary was passed to Chubbie Miller for her to read. It contained a moving account of his last days and messages to those he loved. Among the many messages he had written to his beloved Australian companion were these words: "Chubbie my darling give up flying and settle down!"

It seems likely that when facing an agonising death alone, Lancaster may have reflected on the eventual fate of nearly all the long-distance flyers of that era. Sooner or later they all seemed to die alone in some godforsaken corner of the earth. Maybe he could not face the thought that she, too, could eventually join the long list of the world's lost flyers.

11
Hero of the Tasman

A thin, bespectacled man lay exhausted on a half-inflated rubber raft beside a small muddy water bore in the desolate Queensland Outback.

His drawn features were barely visible beneath the swarm of flies that crawled ceaselessly over his face. A makeshift billy of slimy water boiled over a fire, and nearby a dusty, battered biplane stood silhouetted against the setting sun.

It was 28 January 1930, and the pilot was lost. For the first time since leaving England five weeks earlier — low on fuel, light fading and unable to find Camooweal — he had landed in desperation in search of water.

Sir Francis Chichester, world renowned lone yachtsman, was then making history as the second man to fly solo from England to Australia. Few people realise that his inquisitive spirit and sense of personal challenge were first channelled into flying.

At the age of 18, Chichester emigrated to New Zealand with £10 in his pocket. He tried his hand at farming, gold mining and selling newspapers before finally becoming successful in real estate.

In 1928 he became co-owner of a small aviation business and decided to learn to fly. The following year he was a student at the famous Brooklands Airport School in England. A few months later he was the proud owner of a pilot's licence and a tiny Gipsy Moth aeroplane.

He could think of no better way of returning to New Zealand than to fly there.

At that time, only one man – Bert Hinkler, the famous "Bundaberg Flyer" – had managed to conquer the England-Australia route alone. Many had lost their lives gambling with the overwhelming odds of distance, weather and the unreliability of the aeroplanes of that era.

Chichester's De Havilland aircraft, *Madame Elijah*, was a forerunner of the famous Tiger Moth trainer. A tiny biplane of only 9 metres wingspan, it was powered by an 80-horsepower engine. It had a cruising speed of 128 kph.

Like Hinkler's Avian, it was built as a trainer, ideal for fledgling pilots to practise their circuits and bumps, as landings were affectionately called. But to contemplate crossing the world in such a frail contraption required a man of either great faith and courage or incredible stupidity.

Aware of public sentiment, and sensitive about his lack of experience, Chichester decided to be discreet about his flight and departed unnoticed at 3.15 a.m. on 20 December 1929.

His heavily laden aircraft barely staggered into the air at the end of the Brooklands airstrip. Chichester later discovered that the frozen ground had ripped open a tyre.

Once airborne, he headed for the Channel, keeping his aircraft level by watching the moonlit ground below. He had neither blind flying instruments nor lights aboard.

Over the Channel, cloud obscured the moon and for nearly an hour he flew blind, relying purely on his senses. Just when he feared he was lost, Chichester was lucky enough to pick up the dim outline of the French coast. He landed at Lyons, seven and a half hours after leaving London.

In an hour, his damaged tyre was repaired and the aircraft refuelled. Warmed by a huge omelette washed down by a bottle of red wine, Chichester took off on the next leg to Italy.

Over the Alps he encountered severe turbulence and was fearful that the aircraft's wings would fold up. At times, air currents hurled his plane about so violently that petrol forced from the tank overflow sprayed over his face. Often the Moth was forced down to within a few feet of the peaks.

With nightfall, the air became calm and he landed at Pisa in complete darkness. The waiting Italian Army had neglected to turn the airfield lights on!

He grabbed a couple of hours' sleep, then took off for Sicily. Before daybreak the harrowing effects of his lack of sleep became agonising. Time after time Chichester dozed off. He tried waving his arms, stamping his feet, bouncing up and down in his seat, but all to no avail.

Eventually, by removing his helmet and holding his face to the slipstream, he was able to beat the overpowering desire to sleep. At daybreak, with the sun in his eyes, sleepiness abated, he was afflicted with temporary double vision.

Once on the ground in Sicily, he snatched fifteen minutes' sleep before crossing the Mediterranean and arriving over Africa at sunset. At his destination, Homs, he was again hindered by officials neglecting to light the airfield, so he was forced to carry on to Tripoli.

Here his luck came to an end. Landing in darkness, the aircraft bogged in a wet salt pan and nosed over. Though the aircraft was hardly damaged, his precious propeller was broken.

He had been airborne for twenty-six of the forty hours that had elapsed since leaving England. During the fourteen hours spent on the ground he had only three hours' sleep!

It was three weeks before his aircraft was repaired. During his enforced stopover, four other record-attempting aircraft crashed in North Africa, killing all but one of the pilots.

Every night, Chichester was plagued by a recurring

nightmare. He would dream of being on a flight on which his vision went completely and he sat in the cockpit in fearful darkness waiting for the inevitable crash. He would wake up to find himself out of bed clawing at the windows, trying to escape.

He later recalled that this dream may have been a supernatural warning of what was to come.

In Tripoli, his aircraft repaired, Chichester tested it before setting off. He tried some aerobatics but, as he recalled, "They were so bad I either finished up in spins or barely controllable dives."

The whole Italian aerodrome staff turned out to watch, which only made him more nervous. After thirty minutes of very bad flying he landed to their tumultuous applause.

Before dawn on 9 January 1930, he set off again for distant Australia. Within minutes he was fighting his way through a severe desert sand storm.

Once in the clear he headed across the Nile delta. Landing near Cairo, he flew past a thick column of black smoke rising from the airport. Only minutes earlier, two aircraft had collided in mid-air, killing four pilots.

Crossing the Dead Sea, Chichester flew for hours on end over absolutely featureless desert to the Persian Gulf, then on to Karachi. His maps were primitive by modern standards and much of his route was uncharted. There was no radio or navigation aids. Only he, and the few who flew in that era, could fully appreciate the physical and mental strain of such a flight.

The cramped open cockpit subject to the incessant roar of wind and motor, the searing heat of the desert, the violent turbulence over the mountains, the thousands of kilometres over some of the wildest land in the world, and his life depending on the steady beat of the tiny De Havilland motor . . .

Chichester had fully realised the need for careful servicing of his aircraft. Several times he had to carry out repairs. At a lonely desert fort, Ratbah Wells, he completely dismantled the engine, the whole time watched by a caravan of Arab camel traders. He completed the overhaul after midnight by the light of a small inspection lamp.

Reaching Singapore, Chichester was faced with his first taste of the terrible flying conditions brought about by the monsoon. En route to Indonesia he was continually dogging torrential rain storms and desperately weaving his aircraft among forests of towering storm clouds.

Crossing Indonesia, he was finally faced with an impenetrable barrier of storm clouds. Seeing one clear patch below a heavy black cloud, Chichester darted through. Suddenly his aircraft was enveloped in seemingly solid downpour. Desperately he tried to turn back. Visibility was zero. He struggled to maintain control of the Moth, but it was impossible. His senses told him the aircraft was upside down and diving.

Suddenly he saw waves dead ahead. He was descending vertically. He managed to flatten out only feet above a small bay. Seconds later he emerged from the wall of rain to see his destination ahead.

A series of landings on water-logged airstrips, often enlisting the help of natives to push his aircraft out of the mud, finally brought Chichester to Timor and the dreaded crossing of the Timor Sea. In fact, the long over-water leg that brought disaster to so many pilots was his easiest of the whole trip.

On arriving at Darwin, a few men stood idly by at the airport when he thankfully switched off the motor. Formalities over, Chichester adjourned to the nearest pub. Next morning he headed south across the barren inland for Camooweal.

Chichester recalled this leg as a navigator's nightmare. His map, provided by the Australian Civil Aviation Department, marked all settlements in a grand manner and where he expected a town of maybe 5000 people there would be a house and a couple of sheds. It showed many rivers, but in nine hours' flying Chichester saw none.

Thus, with his arrival at Camooweal overdue and utterly confused, he put down alongside the deserted water bore.

The combination of heat, lack of sleep and worry finally overcame his normal calm and he was panic-stricken. Shaking uncontrollably, he had great difficulty in setting up camp and in carrying even a small container of water. Eventually he dropped with exhaustion and had a fitful night's sleep.

With the new day, his composure returned. By mentally retracing his movements of the previous day he deduced that Camooweal must be within 15 kilometres.

A check of his tank showed thirty minutes of fuel left, and he decided to head south-east. After fifteen minutes of flying he saw buildings ahead. He landed at Rocklands Homestead, just 5 kilometres north of his destination.

Thousands of people at Sydney's Mascot Airport gave Chichester a rousing welcome when, on 31 January 1930, he arrived accompanied by ten aircraft of the New South Wales Aero Club. The crowd was a complete surprise to him and he recalled making one of his worst-ever landings.

On returning to New Zealand he was still plagued by his obsession to do something no one else had yet achieved. Within a few weeks he determined to attempt a round-the-world solo flight. Having already completed a third of the distance he now had to cross the Tasman to Australia and head up via Japan, Alaska and America over the North Atlantic back to England.

But the biggest hurdle was the Tasman. There seemed no way he could equip his Moth with tanks large enough for the fuel required for the 2120-kilometre crossing. A search of New Zealand failed to uncover a suitable larger aircraft. The venture seemed to have become an impossible dream.

One morning, while shaving, Chichester glanced down at a large globe on the table and noticed two tiny dots located in the North Tasman Sea. They represented Norfolk and Lord Howe Islands. Suddenly the answer came. Instead of flying the shortest direct route to Australia he could island-hop. It was nearly twice the distance, but the islands appeared closely enough spaced for the range of his tiny de Havilland Moth.

Following a detailed survey of the route, the airman established the distances that could be covered with a safe fuel margin. The islands' volcanic origin meant they were unlikely to have cleared level areas suitable for landing. No aircraft had yet visited either place.

Thus the only way he could use the islands as refuelling stops was to equip his aircraft with floats and to land in the sea. This was a real risk at Norfolk, which had no sheltered bay: he would have to risk the open sea swell in the lee of the island. Even though Lord Howe had a lagoon there was no way of knowing how rough the water might be on his arrival. The Tasman was well known for its fickle seas and sudden storms.

The search for floats ended when Chichester located a pair of damaged pontoons in the corner of an air force hangar. They were relics of another Moth that had accidentally been dropped 10 metres on to the deck of a warship. Desperately short of money, he approached the government to hire or loan the floats.

At first the Director of Aviation, Wing Commander Grant-Dalton, refused, asking that Chichester forget the flight altogether. Another "lost airman" would set New Zealand aviation back – the public still remembered Hood and Moncrieff who had disappeared on a Tasman flight two years before.

But Chichester would not give up. He felt himself destined to fly the Tasman. "I had to make the flight, and could not escape it," he wrote years later. He applied repeatedly until the authorities finally relented and loaned him the floats.

But his problems were still far from over. How was he going to navigate over open sea for 800 kilometres and then hit a speck in the ocean? Norfolk was a mere 8 kilometres long and 5 kilometres wide. An error of just one degree would mean missing the island by 13 kilometres and over such a distance, with no features on the open sea to help keep a check on his progress, Chichester would be lucky not to have a track error of 10 degrees. That would mean missing by a fatal 130 kilometres. The leg to Lord Howe, less than half the size of Norfolk and 100 kilometres further away, was even worse.

The airman realised that it would be suicide to rely on dead-reckoning navigation — the usual answer to flight over featureless terrain. He must devise some system that would guarantee an accuracy of less than 1 degree.

His theory of sea navigation using a sextant to read the sun was criticised by the experts, who warned him it was impossible for a man flying alone in a bumping aircraft to take accurate readings on the delicate equipment. Refusing to accept their advice, he read every book he could find on the subject, only to find that, even if the readings were accurate, the system devised for ships would not work for aircraft.

He eventually got his first clue to a totally new system of astro-navigation from a seafaring textbook published in 1840. It involved flying a curved path based on "sun-shots" to a spot on the chart 150 kilometres abeam of his destination. Once at that phantom point he would turn at right angles and, keeping the sun exactly at 90 degrees to the aircraft, would home in to the island. It was later to be dubbed "Chichester's theory of the deliberate error" and become the standard navigational technique of Second World War maritime aircraft.

He took off from Auckland Harbour in the pre-dawn gloom of 28 March 1931. With sunset on Norfolk Island expected at 6.45 p.m., Chichester had twelve hours of daylight available. In that time he must cover 960 kilometres and make a refuelling stop at the northern tip of New Zealand, a formidable task in an aircraft with a cruising speed of only 125 kph.

During the two-and-a-half-hour flight to Parengaranga Harbour, the airman made a final check of his sun-shot navigation technique. With the Moth over a known position on the coast, he took a sextant reading and computed his position from the observation. When he compared his findings with the actual position on the chart, Chichester felt a moment of panic. There was a discrepancy of 170 kilometres. Only after reworking his figures did he discover he had forgotten to allow for the known error in his watch. He recalled the problems:

> I felt desperate at thinking of all the blunders of this kind I could make. However, I recovered; the work required extraordinary concentration. It had been easy enough in a car driven at 50 mph by someone else; in a seaplane it was at first difficult to concentrate enough while attending to the five instrument readings, maintaining a compass course, reducing the sun sight, and solving the spherical triangle involved. The 100 mph wind of the propeller slip-stream, which struck the top of my head just above the windshield, made concentrating difficult; so did the pulsating roar from the open exhausts.

The refuelling process at Parengaranga took two and a half frustrating hours. The genial Maoris who rowed out to meet him did not have the prearranged fuel with them. They had not expected he would arrive so early! While they returned to the shore to fetch the tins, the airman sat astride the fuselage eating a bread and jam lunch. When the job was finally completed, Chichester estimated he could still make Norfolk Island before dark . . . but at best he had less than an hour's daylight to spare. As he prepared to start the engine, his smiling refueller asked where the airman was headed. When told the destination was Australia, the Maori shook his head exclaiming, "Py corry! The th' phlurry long way to swim, I tink."

Only after several attempts did Chichester manage to lift the heavily laden Moth from the water. He would later discover that a leaking float had made the aircraft lift many litres of parasite sea water.

As New Zealand slipped astern, the airman carefully scanned the sea's surface, trying to establish a rough wind speed and direction to estimate the aircraft's angle of drift.

By the end of the second hour he had taken two sun observations and was able to establish that a strong tail wind had pushed his groundspeed up to 160 kph.

Conditions were perfect: a cloudless sky and unlimited visibility. The Moth's 80-horsepower Gipsy engine had not missed a beat, and Chichester relaxed, enthralled by the experience. "Ahead stretched the ocean, sparkling under the eye of the sun; no sport could touch this, it was worth almost any price. I seemed to expand with vitality and power and zest," he wrote in his book *The Lonely Sea and the Sky*.

Due to his superb navigation, Norfolk Island came in sight within minutes of the estimated time of arrival. At 5.40 p.m. he made a safe landing on the sea in Cascade Bay. The so-called bay was little more than an indentation in the 100-metre high cliffs that ringed the island. But it afforded the best protection from the heavy south-easterly swell that pounded against the rocks.

Chichester had planned to stay only one night, but the badly leaking float prevented him from taking off next morning and he spent two days repairing it. While on the island he was the guest of the Administrator and stayed in the fortress-like Government House built during Norfolk's early penal colony days. As the first airman to visit the tiny outpost he was warmly welcomed by the islanders, mostly descendants of Fletcher Christian's HMS *Bounty* mutineers.

A heavy swell was running when *Madame Elijah* was lowered back on to the water by a small crane at the Cascade Jetty. With a bare minimum of fuel on board, Chichester took off and flew over to a coral-protected bay on the other side of the island. There he took on fuel and supplies and next morning, April Fools Day, scraped out of Emily Bay bound for microscopic Lord Howe Island.

An hour and a half out he sighted the SS *Makambo* on her monthly supply visit to Norfolk. It was the first ship he had seen since leaving New Zealand and gave him a chance to try out a tiny radio transmitter a friend had fixed in the Moth's cramped cockpit. Chichester had promised to make a number of Morse transmissions during the flight to test the equipment, but with no receiver on board he had no way of telling whether the signals were going out. He tapped out a message to the *Makambo* at a distance of approximately 40 kilometres and was excited to see the ship reply by belching out a huge puff of smoke.

An hour later he was in trouble. Out of nowhere a severe vibration appeared. At first he thought it was the engine, but a careful check of the instruments and exhaust note indicated the Gipsy was running normally. The vibration increased until the airman found the shaking of the whole airframe made it impossible to write his log. Chichester concluded it must be the propeller. Somehow it had got out of balance. He could only carry on and hope the aircraft did not shake to pieces around him.

Later he realised that the aircraft was heading well off course. The vibration had loosened the holding screws of the compass so much that it had moved out of place. Using a small pocket compass, he realigned the one in the aircraft and jammed wads of paper down the side to hold it in position.

Not only did he have an aircraft problem, but now his navigation could be suspect. Chichester forced himself to relax . . . it was time for a meal. He opened a tin of pineapple chunks, delicately spearing the sweet morsels with his navigation dividers, until with the final swig of juice, he tossed the empty can overboard. Feeling less tense he settled back down to the business of navigating.

By the time he approached the turn-off point for Lord Howe, the Moth's dashboard airspeed indicator and both altimeters had given up from the constant vibration. How long could the rigging and airframe continue to take the stress? Rainstorms and lowering clouds added to Chichester's worries.

After six hours and forty minutes flying, he estimated he should be in sight of Lord Howe. Where was the island? Had he miscalculated? With the vibration affecting his instruments and his ability to make accurate sextant sightings anything could have happened. He was just reaching again for something to eat to ease the worry when Chichester sighted a tall jagged mountain emerging from a rain squall dead ahead. It was little Lord Howe Island.

As he approached for landing in the choppy lagoon, the Moth was suddenly caught in a savage downdraft. Equipment was flung around the cockpit. The airman clung on desperately, trying to regain control and stop the aircraft from diving into the water. He was just able to check the violent descent. Eager to escape any further turbulence, Chichester made a hurried landing. The aircraft was moored for the night and the tired airman caught a few hours' fitful sleep.

Before dawn next day, Chichester was awakened suddenly by the noise of a wild storm, with a wind strong enough to strip the roof from the house. By daylight he and his host, P.J. Dingham, were anxiously heading for the lagoon. They arrived to a heart-breaking sight. *Madame Elijah* was upside down in the water with only her tail and part of the floats showing. She looked for all the world ''like a big fish diving into the water''.

During the next forty days on Lord Howe Island a minor miracle took place in an old boat shed under a banyan tree. When the Moth had been dragged from the water, it was a write-off, the only salvageable parts being the fuselage, the floats and the engine. At first Chichester had resigned himself to finishing his Tasman crossing by ship. But after a sleepless night he decided that he would finish the crossing as he had started − solo. Even if meant sailing a small boat. By next morning his plans had progressed even further. He would rebuild the aircraft.

He had no engineering training other than the usual knowledge most pilots picked up along the way. He made an inventory of the parts he would need. Wood, screws, fabric, yarn, rope, paint, new magnetos, the hundreds of items that went into building new wings and refurbishing the rest of the aircraft. While he waited for the next supply ship to arrive he and a handful of unskilled but inventive islanders dismantled, cleaned, checked and rebuilt the engine. When the load of parts finally arrived, Chichester, with the help of islanders skilled only in boat building, and two expert needlewomen, rebuilt and recovered the Moth's wood and fabric airframe. The success of the undertaking was a testament to the airman's genius and sheer determination, and the talents of his friends on Lord Howe.

On the first test flight, the new *Madame Elijah* nearly came to grief when the engine stopped dead shortly after take-off. The problem was soon rectified and after a second (perfect) flight, Chichester took his island assistants into the air on a series of short joyflights. Their first taste of flying was in "their own" aeroplane.

The following day, 10 June 1931, he took off from Lord Howe on the shortest flight of the crossing. Australia was only six hours away and with its size he could not miss! The water conditions, weight and a problem float combined to give the airman some anxious moments getting off the water. *Madame Elijah* was close to a stalled condition when Chichester finally dragged the Moth from the surface, almost clipping a row of palms as it staggered over the shore. Once flying speed had been attained, an elated Chichester climbed slowly into the west and headed for Sydney.

Two hours out the engine began missing badly. The magnetos were playing up. After a while it seemed to clear itself. But no sooner was one problem over than another followed. Then a series of violent storms blocked his path so that Chichester had no alternative other than to press on beneath them. For the next hour he was bombarded by torrential rain, winds and violent turbulence. Once he was forced to within a few metres of the mountainous seas to keep sight of the water. At other times he flew completely "blind" by his instruments as the wall of rain merged with the iron-grey sea. The airman kept telling himself over and over to "keep cool". Eventually he broke out into clear weather, almost blinded by the dazzle of the sun after the blackness of the storm.

The weather steadily improved as he closed in on Australia, and the skies were almost clear when Chichester experienced his final trial – a mysterious meeting with a UFO. He later wrote:

> Suddenly it caught my eye 30 degrees to the left front. Then vivid flashes in several places like the dazzle of a heliograph . . . Then I saw advancing – great heavens – the dull grey-white shape of an airship. Airship! Impossible! However, there was no doubt about it. It nosed towards me like an oblong pearl. Nothing but a cloud or two was visible in the skies for miles. I looked left sometimes catching a flash or a glint there. Turning again to the airship I found it had completely vanished. I screwed my eyes up unable to believe them.

Twisting his head this way and that the puzzled airman banked the Moth from side to side in case the airship was hidden in a blind spot, but it was nowhere to be seen. Just as he was about to settle back on course, it reappeared and flew towards him. He was astonished for, instead of increasing in size, it grew steadily smaller. The gap narrowed until the airship was quite close, when it suddenly became transparent, then vanished.

Alarmed and confused by his meeting with the ethereal airship, Chichester could only continue his flight. He could think of no explanation for the strange phenomenon. In 1931 the world had not yet been bombarded with reports of flying saucers and other UFOs. He wrote: "I felt stranded in solitude. It was intolerable."

Having gone well off course to avoid further storms, *Madame Elijah* made landfall near Jervis Bay, well south of Sydney. The jubilant airman landed in the water close to a group of Australian naval ships and was eventually hoisted on board the aircraft carrier HMAS *Albatross*. There he was made an honoured guest of the Royal Australian Navy.

Six weeks later, Chichester took off from Sydney Harbour to continue his around-the-world flight. He had reached Japan when a crash put an end to his pioneer flying career.

Madame Elijah had just got airborne at Katsura when it collided with telegraph wires stretching between two hills flanking the harbour. The stricken aircraft fell several hundred metres before crashing into the sea wall. Chichester was terribly injured, but miraculously survived the crash, and surgeons managed to save his sight. He did a little flying some years later, but by then he had turned his attention to sailing.

In 1967 he finally accomplished the dream that had eluded him for thirty-six years – the solo circumnavigation of the world. But instead of his Gipsy Moth aircraft *Madame Elijah*, Chichester circled the world single-handed in his yacht he lovingly named *Gipsy Moth*. His voyage captured the imagination of the world and he was knighted by Queen Elizabeth on the deck of his boat. Newspapers called him "a new Elizabethan", "truly the old man of the sea". But a part of him always remained in the air. Before his death in 1972 he said, "I found flying more exciting than sailing, particularly that flight across the Tasman Sea. Evolving a new method of navigation and knowing if it failed you would finish up in the drink. That sort of challenge is what life is made of."

Those words hold the key to Chichester the man. He not only met the challenge of distance, but gambled on the accuracy of his own untried navigation system, and his ability to centre the dancing bubble of a spirit level. This bubble determined the accuracy of the vital sextant readings that aimed *Madame Elijah* at the bullseye islands; readings that all the experts said no man could take in the cockpit of a bouncing aircraft.

But then Sir Francis Chichester was no ordinary man.

12
Australia's Indomitable Airwoman

The sheer frustration of being a golfing widow has driven many a woman to contemplate divorce. But rather than idly bemoan her "widowhood", one young Queensland housewife saw a golden opportunity to take up her own hobby.

While her husband spent his weekends trying to roll a little white ball into a hole in the ground, Lores Bonney learnt to fly.

In a land where the history of early aviation seems always concerned only with the feats of men like Kingsford Smith and Hinkler, the pioneering flights of this adventurous woman have somehow been obscured by the passing years.

Born in South Africa, she married Brisbane leather goods manufacturer Harry Bonney in 1917. Ten years later she had her first taste of flying when her husband's cousin Bert Hinkler took her up in his Avro biplane. While her husband traipsed around the fairways of the Royal Queensland Golf Club, Mrs Bonney secretly learnt to fly at the nearby Eagle Farm Airfield. Her instructor was Charles Matherson.

"I never told my husband until I made my first solo flight," she recalls. "I didn't know what his reaction would be. I phoned him from the aerodrome. He had known about my learning to fly all the time and hadn't let on."

After completing her initial training, Mrs Bonney carried out advanced flying at Archerfield's Royal Aero Club of Queensland, and was awarded a Commercial Pilot's Licence. She was soon the proud owner of a tiny De Havilland Moth biplane she called *My Little Ship*, a gift from her husband.

Over the next five years, this remarkable woman was to set an impressive array of records that, even today, remains unequalled by any Australian woman pilot — and by only a few men.

On 5 January 1932 she created a new Australian record by flying solo from Brisbane to Wangaratta, Victoria, a distance of more than 1600 kilometres, in one day. No mean achievement in an aircraft with a cruising speed of only 128 kph.

Later that year, following several long interstate flights, she decided to fly around Australia. This historic journey, the first by a woman, was completed on 27 September 1932. It was not without incident. Landing at Broome in Western Australia, the Moth got involved with a "willy-willy" and a wing struck the ground on touchdown. Temporary repairs were made, but Mrs Bonney was concerned to feel the aircraft "shivering" as she went on through rough air to Perth. There it was discovered that a wing spar was broken! Following the long Nullarbor crossing, her engine failed near Adelaide and she force-landed in a paddock, but the closest brush with disaster came when flying in formation with a Shell Company photographic plane near Glenrowan. The tail fin of the other aircraft collided with her wing as it passed beneath the Moth. Mrs Bonney was horrified to see the Shell plane go into a spin and crash land below her. To her relief, the occupants scrambled clear and waved her on to Benalla. *My Little Ship*, though damaged, was still flyable, so she carried on and had it repaired after reaching her next stopping point.

Following the flight, a reception was given in her honour by the Royal Aero Club of Queensland. She was also awarded the Qantas trophy for the outstanding performance by any pilot in 1932.

In 1933, confident of her ability to withstand the rigours of long-distance flying, Mrs Bonney decided to go for the big one. At that time no woman had even attempted the hazardous flight from Australia to England. It was recognised as going the hard way, as the direction is against the prevailing winds. When asked why she chose it, Mrs Bonney replied, "Well, everyone else was coming the other way!" She asked Charles Kingsford Smith if he thought a woman could do the flight. He replied somewhat cynically, "Yes, if you've got the guts!" That sort of challenge only added to her determination to try it.

Mrs Bonney put her aircraft in the hands of the Qantas maintenance team at Archerfield and requested a complete overhaul of the Moth. Realising that to have any chance of completing the flight she must also be able to service its "Gipsy" engine, she took a practical course with the engineers doing the job.

Day after day she would arrive at the hangar, change into greasy overalls and help with the overhaul.

Setting tappets, cleaning and gapping oiled spark plugs, adjusting magnetos, clearing blocked fuel lines, the determined woman learned the scores of maintenance jobs that would be needed to keep the little four-cylinder motor purring away smoothly over the 20 000 kilometres to England. As she watched and learned every new operation, she made detailed notes to take with her on the flight.

Mrs Bonney had entered an entirely all-male domain at the servicing hangar and at first the bemused men rather resented her intrusion. But as time passed they came to respect and admire her determination and will to learn. No job was too menial and they were amazed to see a woman quite unconcernedly plunging her hands into the deep containers of cleaning solvent and oil baths to extract parts of the engine being cleaned and oiled before reassembly.

The ever-present practical jokers had a heyday at her expense, but they too eventually gave up in admiration of her desire to learn and willingness to tackle any task.

When the tiny biplane was finally reassembled and ready for its long flight, Mrs Bonney knew her aircraft inside out and felt confident that she could handle any minor mechanical problem that might otherwise have meant an untimely end to her pioneering attempt.

On 12 April 1933 she took off from Brisbane. Ahead lay more than 20 000 kilometres over some of the most savage land on earth. Even today the flight is considered a challenge in a modern light aircraft with sophisticated equipment. Forty years ago aircraft were still in their infancy. With sketchy maps, no radio navigation aids, inadequate blind flying instruments, primitive servicing facilities and meteorological services, the flight was like a game of Russian roulette. Mrs Bonney carried no radio and had only a simple compass by which to navigate.

At Charleville, hotelier Harry Corones presented her with a bottle of whisky. Every pioneering pilot he knew of had carried one on board for the dreaded crossing of the lonely shark-infested Timor Sea. At least a couple had overindulged in "Dutch courage" to keep their nerve, he confided. She carefully stowed the bottle away, determined not to use it.

To be on the safe side, Mrs Bonney carried a small rubber dinghy tied to the Moth's undercarriage. It is doubtful if it would have been of any use in the case of a ditching.

The flight from Darwin to Singapore went without incident. At each landing point she cabled back news of her progress to Australia and newspapers published daily bulletins on the flight.

On 20 April, between Singapore and Victoria Point, she was trapped by a violent tropical storm. Surrounded by black clouds and buffeted by torrential rain, Mrs Bonney was forced to make an emergency landing on Bang Biang Island. *My Little Ship* had just touched down on the small beach when a buffalo ran out into its landing path. Mrs Bonney pushed hard on the rudder to swerve and avoid colliding with the animal, but in doing so a wheel sank into soft sand and a wing struck the water. The biplane flipped over on to its back in the surf. The cockpit ended up under water and Mrs Bonney, upside down, held her breath as she struggled to undo her harness. She finally scrambled clear and reached the beach. Except for minor injuries to her forehead and right hand, she was miraculously unhurt.

The island was inhabited by Malays who were initially too scared to come near her. She eventually overcame their timidity and persuaded them to help her right the waterlogged aircraft and float it up on to the beach.

When the Moth was finally secured above the high-water point, it was a sorry sight indeed. Both the upper and lower mainplanes were extensively damaged. The tail fin was broken and the laminated wooden propeller shattered. Much of the damage to the fabric-covered wings had been at the hands of the over-eager people as they had swarmed around the upturned aircraft attempting to lift it out of the pounding surf.

As Mrs Bonney sadly surveyed the aircraft, sea water dribbling from a score of openings in the fuselage, she realised that there was no hope of repairing it on this prim-itive island.

As the sun set, she was led, utterly exhausted, to a large communal hut in the nearby village. Here, in company of a swarm of natives, she was to spend the night. Within moments of her arrival, a tiny native woman took the tired and bewildered pilot under her wing, and became her constant companion and protector. Even though they were unable to communicate by more than sign language, Mrs Bonney sensed very quickly the concern and care of her newfound friend and quickly christened her "S.O.S." (Soul of Sympathy).

Inside the highest hut, rows of curious eyes watched her every movement. Eventually, to gain some peace and privacy, she strung a line from wall to wall at the far end of the barrack-like room. On it she hung her spare clothing to form a screen. The odour of sweating bodies and cooking fish was so overpowering that she eventually had to burn mosquito coils to overcome its nauseating effects.

During her stay on Bang Biang Island, "S.O.S." followed Mrs Bonney everywhere and with a few angry words kept the occasional over-inquisitive villager at a respectable distance.

One of the first items of kit the airwoman recovered from the emergency supplies in her battered aircraft was a small cooking stove fuelled with methylated spirit tablets, and her survival rations. The locals stared in wonder each time she lit her tiny stove and prepared her own meals. They considered her chewing gum, which she had distributed among them, a great delicacy. It was not until after she had left the island that Mrs Bonney noticed that her reserve supplies of methylated spirit tablets, which looked remarkably like the pieces of gum, had been stolen! It is probable that the village medicine man had a number of unexplainable stomach complaints on his hands following her departure!

It was nearly three days before an anxious world learned that the Australian airwoman was safe. Some locals had paddled to the mainland and then trekked 50 kilometres by night through the jungle to bring two tin miners to her aid.

When the tin miners finally arrived they were surprised to find that the local native District Commissioner also had heard of her crash, and with his family had already reached the island to help her.

Mrs Bonney recalled that following the crash she finally opened the bottle of whisky – to sterilise her cut hand! True to form, she did not waste her time on the island. When the mining company launch arrived they found her busy learning Malay from the natives.

The damaged aircraft was shipped on a sampan to Victoria Point. Learning that the nearest suitable repair facilities were in Calcutta she embarked on the S.S. *Juna* with the battered Moth as deck cargo. She told doubting pressmen, "Even if it takes me ten years I am determined to reach England."

A month later she left Calcutta and crossed India. All went well across the wastes of Persia and Turkey, but she was plagued by bad weather as she reached Bulgaria. Mrs Bonney planned her final leg to be non-stop from Budapest to London, but again she encountered appalling weather. After flying blind in circles to find a way out of the storms, she force-landed in a field in Czechoslovakia and was detained for landing without a permit! The Czechs ransacked her aircraft before finally letting her continue on.

At Cologne, Mrs Bonney went to turn on final approach when she felt the control stick jam solid. She landed safely − "by the grace of God" − and climbed out of her aircraft thoroughly shaken. After a detailed examination, sceptical engineers pronounced there was nothing wrong. Determined to disprove their theories about "hysterical women pilots", she checked the controls herself, and eventually found a crushed tin of bully beef lodged under the base of the front control column!

On 21 June she landed at London's Croydon Airport. In recognition of being the first woman to make the flight, she was awarded the MBE.

During the period of Mrs Bonney's flight, an aviation-minded world had received news of several less fortunate pilots. Captain Lancaster flew to his death in the Sahara, an Italian pioneer and two Russians were lost en route to Australia, and New Zealand's Jean Batten was missing for ten days on her flight from London to her homeland.

Not content to rest on her laurels, Mrs Bonney decided to make an even longer and more challenging flight. She wanted to be the first person to link Australia and South Africa by air. For this monumental flight she obtained a German-built Klemm monoplane with a range of 1600 kilometres. She called it *My Little Ship II*.

On 19 April 1937, she left Archerfield bound for Cape Town. Her early progress was punctuated by incredibly bad weather. To reach Surabaja she was forced to fly within a few metres of the sea in teeming rain and near zero visibility. En route to Batavia she was again forced down to tree-top height and later crossed and recrossed the channel between Banka Island and Sumatra five times before finally threading her way between the storms.

Singapore, Bangkok, Rangoon on to Calcutta . . . all the way plagued by an incessant run of tropical storms. Across India the searing heat became her new problem. At one stage it was so intensely hot in the cockpit that she could not put her hand on the throttle. Landing at Agra she literally fell out of the aircraft, overcome by heat prostration.

Over Iran, headwinds slowed down the Klemm to a mere 80 kph. Nevertheless, on arrival at Basra, Mrs Bonney had covered 14 622 kilometres in eighty-seven hours' flight time.

From Baghdad, over hundreds of kilometres of desolate scorching deserts, the Klemm droned on. Here failure of the motor would have resulted in almost certain death. Finally she crossed the Suez Canal and its oasis of cultivation. Heading south past Khartoum, she had a major setback. At Juba, in East Africa, she damaged the tail section landing in turbulence. There were no repair facilities for hundreds of kilometres and the flight seemed doomed to failure.

Here again this remarkable woman's indomitable will took over. She refused to give up and eventually was lucky enough to track down a small detachment of Royal Air Force personnel passing through the town. Within minutes she had enlisted their help.

The aircraft was manhandled from the airstrip to the banks of the river Nile. A flat-topped river barge was moored close in to the low-lying shore and the Klemm slowly inched by sweating Arabs and airmen up a pair of ramps on to the deck. Once on board, its wings were folded back along the fuselage and a rough wooden canvas-covered hangar was erected to protect the crippled air-craft.

With the arrival of the paddlesteamer that regularly plied the reaches of the upper Nile, Mrs Bonney took passage to Khartoum. As the ancient riverboat set out, its deck was crammed with boxes and baskets of vegetables, fruit, poultry, cattle, noisy Arabs and yelling crewmen, like some great floating market place chugging down the placid river to Khartoum. Swinging at the stern, under the receding umbrella of black smoke from the steamer's tall funnel, followed the flat-topped barge carrying the solitary aircraft.

After a colourful five-day journey they arrived at the city, immortalised over fifty years earlier when General Gordon and his force were massacred by the Mahdi's force. There willing RAF mechanics soon repaired *My Little Ship II*.

Across Tanganyika and Northern Rhodesia she battled violent turbulence over the towering mountains and bone-shaking airpockets rising from hundreds of dense bushfires.

At Livingstone, a lovely place that reminded her of being home in Queensland, the flight almost ended in disaster. She had just lined up for take-off when the undercarriage collapsed and the aircraft heeled over on one wing. Petrol streamed from a split tank. "I was lucky, for in another few seconds I would have given the plane full throttle, and it would surely have turned over," Mrs Bonney reflected.

A badge presented to her by the South African Air Force unit in Pretoria, her birthplace, became a treasured memento of the flight. Finally, after a treacherous crossing of the Hex River Mountains, the little aircraft touched down to a perfect landing at Cape Town. In 181 hours' flight time the Queensland aviatrix had flown an unbelievable 29 088 kilometres!

"It never struck me that I would not make it, being a fatalist," Mrs Bonney said recently. "I wasn't worried one scrap. I had faith in God, in myself and in my aeroplane." She recalls how one pilot roared with laughter when he learned she could not even drive a car; her husband considered motor cars too dangerous!

Mrs Bonney dreamed of making one more long-distance flight to London via the Aleutians and New York. But it was not to be. Shortly before the outbreak of war, her beloved *My Little Ship II* was destroyed in a fire in Qantas No. 2 hangar at Archerfield. With the outbreak of hostilities three months later, her flying career came to an end.

Following the war, and after the death of her husband, Mrs Bonney moved from Brisbane into a beautiful Japanese-style home overlooking the Pacific Ocean at Miami, Queensland. She always flew as Mrs "Harry" Bonney, in respect of her late husband who so helped and unselfishly encouraged her flying ambitions. Following the war she withdrew completely from the world of aeroplanes. It was too painful to be around them and not be able to fly.

Recognition of her pioneering flights finally came from the United States, where she was invited to attend the unveiling of a plaque bearing her name on a memorial wall carrying the names of the world's great aviation pioneers.

But although she had given up the world of flying, it was impossible to suppress her inquisitive spirit. At an age when most women are content to attend morning teas, do a little knitting, or if really ambitious take an overseas tour on a luxury liner, Mrs Bonney took off on another adventure. This time, accompanied by a French guide and local helpers, she explored the upper reaches of the Amazon river by motor boat and canoe. The areas they explored are rarely visited by white people and the indigenous tribes are unpredictable.

For most of her life she had felt a great admiration for people of the East and their lifestyle. It was not surprising that her next adventure would take her back to that part of the world. During a number of extended visits to Japan she studied under a leading master of the exquisite art of bonsai. An expert, by occidental standards, she devoted hours daily to growing and tending the miniature Japanese trees and plants.

Her post-war travels were always by sea. "I hate being in an aeroplane as a passenger. It's like being in a cage."

In the early 1930s, all eyes seemed to be on the great pioneering airmen of the Commonwealth. Australians have always appeared in the past to make heroes only of their men and chronicle their achievements. And yet in England, Amy Johnson became a national idol. Ask any American about Amelia Earheart. Hardly a single New Zealander could not recount the flights of Jean Batten.

Ask your neighbours about Mrs Bonney – they'll probably just scratch their heads.

It is paradoxical that here in Australia, historically one of the world's most airminded nations, we somehow nearly forgot Lores Bonney – one of the world's, and Australia's, great pioneer pilots.

Footnote: On Australia Day 1991, Lores Bonney, aged 94 years, finally received long-overdue recognition from her home land, when she was awarded an Order of Australia.

13
Airman, Inventor, Adventurer

On 21 April 1918, the most famous fighter pilot of all time, Manfred von Richthofen – the dreaded "Red Baron" – crashed to his death in France. A group of excited Australian soldiers were the first at the site of the mangled remains of the scarlet-red Fokker. They were well aware that the body they carried from the wreckage was that of the respected German ace. It was curious, they thought, that beneath his leather flying jacket he should be wearing a British Sidcot flying suit.

Within hours, the news of his death raced around the battlefront.

To one man, the unusual details of Richthofen's clothing was of particular interest. For Sidney Cotton, a Queensland flying with the Royal Naval Air Service, had designed and produced the revolutionary flying suit, worn gratefully by Allied airmen in the freezing skies of two world wars.

The story of Sidney Cotton, born near Proserpine in 1894, is an incredible series of adventures linked by the thread of his greatest love – flying. Fighter pilot, pioneer, undercover agent, intelligence expert, businessman, inventor . . . his achievements justly earned him the title of the "Magnificent Elizabethan".

In 1910 the Cotton family booked passage to England on the steamer *Waratah*. It had been decided that Sidney and his brothers would benefit from a few years of schooling in the "motherland".

At the last minute they were unable to make the sailing date and took a later ship. It was just as well, for en route for Cape Town the *Waratah* disappeared with all hands. The fate of the missing liner still remains one of the sea's great mysteries.

In England, Sidney Cotton saw his first aeroplane when the pioneering aviator Colonel Samuel Cody force-landed into the tree tops whilst performing a display near the Cottons' home. The young man was so excited by the new-fangled machine that he began to visit Brooklands Airfield daily, "just to get close to the bits of wood, wire and fabric that passed as aeroplanes".

Cotton recalled years after, "I remember I could not understand why the pilots kept pulling out little boxes and striking matches, until I was told that they were holding the match up to test the strength of the wind for flying." In those days a breeze that would blow out a burning match was too much for all but the most daring and skilful aviator!

The inventive young Australian built a succession of model aeroplanes, each a little more refined and successful than the last. His final design was over two metres in wingspan, built of bamboo and silk, and powered by a small petrol engine. It flew well — in fact, too well; on its maiden powered flight, it climbed steadily and disappeared over the horizon, never to be found. Six months' work for a single flight.

Two years later the family returned to Australia and settled at "Hidden Vale", a property near Brisbane. Cotton's father hoped his eldest son would emulate his own love for the land and accordingly arranged for him to become a jackeroo on Dalkeith Station in New South Wales.

It soon became obvious to owner Fred McMaster that his new employee's heart was not really in the job. He found that young Cotton was interested in a career in engineering and had designed a small touring car. "All right.

You go down to Sydney and get all the materials you need and come back here and build it. Charge everything to my account," he told the wildly elated young man. It was probably the generosity and advice of the perceptive Fred McMaster that launched Sidney Cotton on his amazing career, for his father, who dearly wanted him to follow in his footsteps and become a station owner, resisted talk of any other career.

Nine months later, the truant jackeroo had built the first all-Australian light car. He was 19 years old and had received no formal engineering training. The Queensland manager of the Willys Overland Car Company was so impressed with its revolutionary chassis, suspension and drive design that he had his factory produce a special streamlined body for it. The final drive system to the rear wheels was virtually identical to one used years later in England by Frazer Nash cars. With the completion of the car, Sidney's mind was soon to be occupied by a new turn of events. The First World War had enveloped Europe.

For months he battled with his unwilling father to allow him to join up. It was only when his 21st birthday approached that his father finally realised that Sidney would leave anyway. Agreement was reached and passage booked for England.

Early in 1915 he reached Southampton and within days had enlisted in the Royal Naval Air Service.

In the early days of the war, flying training was an imperfect art — mainly one of trial and error where those who did not kill or maim themselves gained their flying badge. Few pilots reaching the front line had amassed more than twenty hours of total flying, and the basic flying "ticket" was usually granted after a mere five or so hours.

Sidney Cotton probably established an all-time record when he gained the coveted ticket on the first day he climbed into an aircraft. Due to a misunderstanding, a testing officer picked the young Australian for his ticket test flight, not realising that Cotton had not even commenced his training course. The flying course consisted of a succession of short hops (flights of a few hundred metres), in which the student gained the "feel" of the aircraft controls. They were performed solo, in aircraft with a couple of spark plugs removed from the engine to prevent it from lifting more than a few metres off the ground.

Cotton had been scheduled, on that day, to carry out the first of these flights. One can imagine his confusion and consternation when the dreaded test officer walked him over to a two-seater Maurice Farman Longhorn.

He was given one quick demonstration flight, sitting in the back seat and leaning forward over the pilot's shoulder to observe how he controlled the noisy, shaking contraption. In those days dual-controlled aircraft had not yet been thought of.

It seemed only minutes before they were back on the ground and the young student was blithely told, "Okay, you can take her up by yourself now"! As he strapped in, too confused and scared to own up to the mistaken identity, he vaguely heard the instructor's briefing: "Push the throttle fully open and, when you get to about 40 miles an hour, ease back on the stick until the machine leaves the ground. Now off you go then, and good luck!" Young Cotton was going to need it. It was too late to back out now.

Ten minutes later, Sidney Cotton was back safely on the ground. More by luck than good judgment, he had completed the prescribed figure-of-eight, "split-arse" turn and landing within a marked area. The landing had taken two attempts before he was safely down.

To his amazement, he was congratulated and awarded his prized ticket. The testing officer never found out the truth. Cotton recounted years after that the incident taught him how far it was possible to go on sheer bluff. He added, however, that he was lucky to survive the first few minutes until he got the feel of the machine. Three days later he was posted for advanced training. Shortly after, with a grand total of five hours solo to his credit, he was a member of a squadron patrolling the English Channel! Such was the madness of aerial warfare in those early days. Little wonder the average life expectancy of a pilot on the Western Front was less than a month!

The flying suit was devised by pure chance. British pilots in their open cockpits suffered agony in the cold winter skies over France. Cotton and his fellow squadron pilot, Charles Kingsford Smith, were no exception.

He was tinkering with the engine of his snow-laden Sopwith fighter on a particularly cold, foggy day. To protect himself he had put on a set of grease-covered overalls. An alert was called and the squadron was airborne in minutes. Two hours later the frozen pilots were thawing out in their mess. Someone remarked, "Cotton, you don't seem to be cold at all. Why's that?" Cotton thought for a moment. He was puzzled. In the rush to get airborne he had not been able to get into his flying gear. "That's funny, I was simply wearing my dirty overalls," he replied.

He later realised that the thick coating of oil and grease had turned them into an air-tight bag and trapped his body heat. Grasping that he had the basis of a new type of flying suit, Cotton took leave and headed for London. He arranged for a clothing manufacturer to make up several test suits to his design. They were fur-lined and had an outer layer of light waterproof material. But the key to their amazing warmth lay in the insulating layer of airproof silk sandwiched in between. His names formed the basis of the "Sidcot" trademark under which he registered his design. The famous suits warmed Alcock and Brown as they crossed the Atlantic in 1919 and hardly a man who flew with the RAF in the Second World War did not at some time wear one.

A patriot to the core, he accepted no money from the design, evolved as it was to assist the war effort.

Before the Armistice in 1918, Cotton had introduced numerous other innovations. His De Havilland 4 biplane was the first Allied aircraft to be camouflaged. He also devised specially mounted upward firing Lewis guns for the same machines to take advantage of the weak defensive position directly beneath the giant German Zeppelins. His own Sopwith "one-and-a-half strutter" sported an extra rear-ward-firing machine gun for defensive action.

In 1917 he was posted to a special unit at Hendon, test-ing new machines and equipment. Here he evolved a scheme for a flight of bombers to raid Berlin and carry on to land in Russia. Berlin was outside the return range of Allied bombers. But Cotton had found that by carrying out modification to the DH4, including fitting a less thirsty en-gine, the aircraft could reach the Russian lines. He put his plan to the Admiralty. It was approved and he was relieved of all other duties to organise the raid. Work on the aircraft and special crew training had just got under way when to Cotton's dismay the Admiralty ordered one of the un-modified aircraft with an untrained pilot, on another spe-cial long-distance flight. It was to destroy a Zeppelin at Wilhelmshaven.

Believing the order to be some sort of mistake, Cotton informed Headquarters that neither crew nor machine were capable of carrying out the mission. To his amaze-ment, the Admiralty still insisted the flight take off. The Australian refused to order the flight; it was tantamount to sending the men to certain death, he argued. The flight was ordered into the air by a commodore overruling Cot-ton.

As predicted, the aircraft ran out of fuel over the North Sea, but miraculously the exhausted crew were picked up by a passing cruiser three days later − though not before a flying boat searching for the drowned aircraft was lost at sea.

Following the debacle, Cotton was severely repri-manded for challenging orders. As punishment he was re-lieved of his special appointment for his alleged disobedience. The senior officer who had made the incred-ible decision to order the abortive raid was not one to admit to his mistake. Cotton was to be the scapegoat. In his typical forthright manner, the young officer retorted, "If this is the way the Admiralty are going to run the war I will resign my commission."

This was to be the first of many run-ins he was to have with officialdom and the often near-criminal ignorance of senior military officers and government officials. His straightforward Australian approach was not suited to the devious infighting and deception commonly practised at the top of the ladder.

Despite pleas from brother officers, Cotton left the RNAS shortly before the war ended and volunteered immediately for the Royal Australian Flying Corps. He was turned down cold. The reason, he found out years after, was that the Admiralty had marked his records with the statement: "He is of difficult temperament and unsuitable for employment in uniformed service." The Australian authorities of 1918 were more dependent on, and constricted by, the "home country" and felt they could not ignore such advice.

In 1919 he returned to Australia and the family property, but was unable to settle down. A year later he was back in England preparing a De Havilland aircraft to fly to Australia. The news came that the Smith brothers had already beaten him to it. He made a quick change of plans and set off from Hendon, bound for Cape Town. The flight ended when the plane overturned in a beach landing in southern Italy.

In 1920 Cotton moved to Canada to pioneer aerial spotting for the Newfoundland sealing fleet. Forming his own company, he set up base at Botwood. Here he operated a fleet of primitive war surplus aircraft and had to overcome innumerable problems flying off the frozen lakes – and later ice floes – in the semi-frozen seas off the coast.

To keep the struggling company alive, operations were diversified to include aerial photographic survey for map-making. Also, after a long and frustrating battle with antiquated bureaucracy, he managed to convince the New-foundland government that aircraft could carry the mails faster and more economically than dog sleds. He eventually won a contract to link the island with the mainland.

During their second winter sealing season, the aircraft were having to range farther and farther out to sea in search of the elusive mammals. Even under ideal conditions, the aircraft were notoriously unreliable. Flights were going as far as 300 kilometres out to sea over the ice floes and every pilot was aware of the risk involved. It was estimated that a pilot landing in the super-chilled water would be dead within a minute. If he was lucky to make an ice floe, he might survive a few hours. Yet, though a large number of partial and total engine failures occurred, the company never lost a pilot.

Late in the season of 1923, Cotton was himself 375 kilometres from land when the engine of his Martinsyde started missing badly. "I suddenly realised what a fool I had been. I had been taking these sort of risks for three years," he wrote later. "So far I had been plain lucky, but now the prospect of a freezing death stared me in the face."

As he nursed the slowly failing engine along, Cotton thought of how he had battled, with only limited success, to convince the sealing companies of the value of aircraft, of how the airmail contracts appeared stifled by political bumbling and were threatened by corruption. At that moment it hardly seemed worth having his life hanging in the balance on a spluttering engine. "I made a vow that if I ever got back to land I would give up spotting and, unless I got constructive support from the government, would sell out and leave Newfoundland for good."

Somehow he managed to coax the stricken aircraft back to safety. True to his promise, he sold the business, netting a meagre $25 000 for his three years of heartbreaking labour. But it was his knowledge and great experience of flying over that savage area of Canada that led to his next adventure.

Early on 8 May 1927, two French pilots, Nungesser and Coli, left Paris in their plane *White Bird*. Their destination was New York. They were seen crossing the Irish coast late that day and then they vanished. There were reports that they had been sighted over Newfoundland. Cotton was on business in the United States where he was handling the Canadian promotion of a new snow tractor. The Dupont family — American industrialists of French descent — asked him to mount a search for the missing pilots. In two months Cotton searched 24 000 square kilometres of Newfoundland in his Fokker monoplane. Then vague reports from Ireland that the plane had been seen to crash in the sea near the coast dashed all hopes. The search was called off. For thirty-four years their fate remained a mystery. Then, in 1961, an instrument panel believed to be off the *White Bird* was fished up by a lobsterman off the coast of Maine. The gallant Frenchmen had come pitifully close to making the treacherous east-west crossing.

In 1931, Cotton received another urgent plea, this time from Samuel Courtauld, the synthetics magnate. His nephew, Augustine, a member of the British Arctic Air Route Expedition, was stranded on the ice cap. Would he organise a relief expedition? Young Courtauld had volunteered to stay alone manning a tiny weather station 2500 metres up on the Arctic ice cap. The group had run short of food and decided that there was only enough to support one man.

After four months alone in his tent, now a metre or so beneath the snow surface, the young scientist was almost out of food. An air search had failed to relocate his camp and relief parties had been forced back by blizzards. Trapped in complete darkness, his physical and mental condition were critical.

Under Cotton's direction, three aircraft, the Icelandic

steamer *Dettifoss* and two ground parties converged on the area. Two months after receiving the industrialist's call for help, a ground party found his nephew. A ventilation pipe jutting through the snow and a tattered Union Jack were all that showed of the entombed camp.

Calling down the shaft, the amazed rescuers were over-joyed to hear a weak reply. Courtauld had used his last candle and the life-giving primus stove had run out of fuel that morning. He had been quietly awaiting death!

On returning to England, Cotton reassembled the air-craft he had taken to the Arctic. On its first flight the engine disintegrated soon after take-off and he and his wife narrowly escaped death in the crash landing. Prior to getting the message of Courtauld's rescue, he had been preparing to take off in the same aircraft to cross the Denmark Strait. Had he got airborne that day, the faulty engine would have packed up over the icy sea. "We would not have had a chance," Cotton recalled.

Throughout the 1930s, photography was becoming increasingly popular. To this new and challenging field Cotton turned his drive and imagination. Heading the Dufay-Color company, he pioneered the development of colour photography.

In 1938 a mysterious phone call led him back to flying. British Intelligence was looking for a private pilot prepared, by means of clandestine aerial photography, to gather information on military targets in Germany, Italy and the Middle East. War was looming on the horizon. Cotton often flew on business throughout Europe in his twin-engined Lockheed. It was an ideal cover. He immediately agreed to help and, with ex-RAF co-pilot Flight Lieutenant "Shorty" Longbottom, commenced operations in February 1939.

For the next six months he crisscrossed Europe and the Middle East, his specially concealed cameras recording details of Axis military and industrial installations. Often he was inspected by curious military aircraft. Once over the Siegfried Line a German Messerschmitt fighter rushed up to intercept the Lockheed. Cotton had not forgotten his wartime skills and by cunningly using the sun he escaped over the French border.

Cotton's most audacious spy flight took place right under the eyes of the Luftwaffe. While on a "business visit" to Berlin, he had made friends with Field Marshal Hermann Goering's business manager. Through him he was introduced to the Commandant of the city's Tempelhof Airport.

Commandant Bottger expressed his keen interest in taking a flight in Cotton's "kolossal Lockheed", to which the Australian eagerly agreed. Though nagged by the fear that he was being set up for a Gestapo trap, the chance of doing some local flying outside the strictly enforced air lanes was too good to miss, especially if he could take photographs at the same time! Prior to leaving England he had adapted his hidden wing-mounted Leica cameras to take 250-exposure rolls of film. The cameras were now loaded and shot by electric motors, normally used for motor car windshield wipers. Cotton's self-concocted system was operated by a tiny button concealed under his pilot seat.

Remembering that the Allies were particularly interested in targets in the Mannheim area of the Rhine River – an area banned to all but German military aircraft – Cotton took the plunge: "I had a favourite aunt who always raved about the beautiful Rhine at Mannheim," he declared blandly. "I should like to fly down there." Next day the Gestapo and Luftwaffe authorities gave their permission.

The Lockheed's leisurely flight path took the plane over numerous airfields and military establishments. As the unsuspecting Commandant sat alongside him in the co-pilot's seat Sidney Cotton casually dangled one hand on the edge of his seat. With the slightest of finger pressure he took shot after shot.

As they passed over one particularly conspicuous military base, the insouciant aerial spy set the cameras going again then blushingly hid his eyes with his hands. "I'm sure I am not supposed to see that," he joked to the Commandant, who in return laughed heartily. Cotton mentally blessed his non-existent aunt.

On the return flight to London he pulled off yet another daring trick. Taking advantage of cloud build-ups, Cotton "got lost", strayed well north of the air corridor, and photographed the German defence installations along the infamous Siegfried Line.

Back home the invaluable film was processed. The new automatic Leica system had worked perfectly. As Cotton said, "Of course. The cameras were German made!"

During these flights he thought up many innovations that drastically improved the quality of these photographs and their interpretation.

War was only a few weeks away when he headed off on one of his last intelligence missions; his destination – Berlin. Under cover of establishing a Dufay-Color agency in Germany, he landed at Tempelhof Airport. The aircraft was immediately surrounded by jack-booted Nazi soldiers. Cotton slowly shut down the engines . . . the game was up! Anticipating their immediate arrest, Cotton and his co-pilot stepped out of the aircraft. To their amazement, the soldiers were formed in a guard of honour and saluted the two airmen. Their host, it turned out, was Commandant Botlger.

While in Berlin, Cotton gathered that Hermann Goering had different views on the impending war to those held by Hitler. On the spur of the moment he invited the Marshal to fly with him to England for an informal meeting with Prime Minister Chamberlain. Goering accepted! Cotton hurried back to London and, through Lord Halifax, the meeting was arranged for the end of August.

He then returned to Berlin to find the city echoing to the sounds of marching troops. For two days, amid growing tension, he waited for Goering's arrival. Then he heard the news that Germany and Russia had signed a non-aggression pact. Word arrived from Goering that a meeting was off. It was too late — war was inevitable.

Cotton stayed on, hoping to gather further information that would be of help to British Intelligence. His German friend begged the flyers to leave. If they didn't get out soon, the authorities would not allow them to leave and they would be interned for the duration of the war. Still Cotton hung on. Then a prearranged cable arrived from his headquarters in England: "Mother very ill and asking for you. Mary". It was time to leave.

The parking areas of the airport were crammed with Messerschmitt fighters as they taxied the Lockheed out for take-off. Influential Nazi friends had wangled special permission for his return flight.

Once airborne, the flyers audaciously refitted their Leica cameras in the secret windows. They photographed the German fleet at Wilhelmshaven on the way home! The customs officer at London greeted them with "Where from?" "Berlin," Cotton replied. "Left it a bit late, haven't you?" came the reply. Theirs was the last civilian plane out of Berlin.

During the war, Cotton took his photographic and flying skills to the Royal Air Force. Once again it took a supreme example of the unorthodox Sidney Cotton magic to win military acceptance of his then-revolutionary ideas.

Within days of war being declared, he was approached by Air Vice-Marshal Richard Peck, the RAF's Director of Operations, for advice on aerial photographic techniques. It transpired that the Air Force's photo-reconnaissance squadrons, equipped with slow-flying Blenheim bombers and antiquated cameras, had been trying for weeks to photograph seaport targets on the occupied Dutch coast. So far they had not taken one worthwhile picture.

"Give me a fast aircraft and I'll get them for you," was the typical Cotton reply.

But the RAF were not about to have some upstart civilian do the job for them. In vain he tried to convince the group of senior officers present that their whole photographic system was outdated and needed complete overhauling. Intent only on picking his brains and refusing to employ him in uniform (shades of the First World War Navy report?) they arranged for him to help brief the RAF pilots the next day.

His frustration and anger at their short-sighted stupidity led to his next move. An hour after leaving the conference, he took off in his aircraft from Heston Aerodrome. He was supposedly on a "local" flight. Reaching the coast he set off across the North Sea for Holland. Soon he was dodging in and out of cloud at 3300 metres over the ports of Flushing and Ymuiden, with one eye on the ground and the other looking out for German fighters.

By late that night he had processed an album full of perfect enlargements of the target areas.

The planned briefing at 10 a.m. next morning was attended by a host of senior officers and RAF crews. For half an hour the meeting proceeded on similar lines to the previous day. Then Cotton dropped his bombshell. Casually throwing the album on the table he quietly asked Air Vice-Marshal Peck, "Are these the sort of photos you want?"

Those around the table studied them carefully. "These are first class but we couldn't expect this sort of quality in wartime. When did you take them?"

"That was when I pulled the pin," he recalled. "I said, 'At 3.15 p.m. yesterday'!" For a moment there was a stunned silence, then the room exploded with angry and indignant voices. Cotton was astounded to hear accusations of "flaunting authority . . . misbehaving . . . defying the military . . . ought to be arrested . . ." thrown at him. After a few moments he stood up, turned on his heel and walked slowly from the room. He slammed the door behind him.

Next morning the Chief of the Air Staff, Air Chief Marshal Sir Cyril Newall, called Cotton. "The RAF will never live down what you did yesterday," he said, "but between ourselves I congratulate you on your audacity. We needed those pictures desperately. Will you come and see me? I want you to tell me what is wrong with the RAF's photographic section."

The perceptive Air Chief Marshal realised that other senior officers in the Operations Branch would never forgive Cotton for upstaging them. And after talking with the outspoken Australian he was certain that few of them would fit in with his unorthodox method of getting the job done.

Thus it was that, following consultation with Sir Winston Churchill, the ex-military outcast was asked to form his own Top Secret Special Unit, answerable only to the Chief of Operations and bypassing normal red-tape channels. Among Cotton's handpicked RAF pilots was his old co-pilot "Shorty" Longbottom.

His unorthodox methods achieved brilliant results, but were to persistently run him foul of interservice jealousies and the stagnant thinking of many "old-school" senior officers. His inventive mind was responsible for the "tear-drop" window which greatly improved a pilot's vision — over 100 000 were made during the war. His special "Cottonising" process increased the speed of his photo-recce Spitfires by 65 kph and was used on other special purpose RAF aircraft. The camouflage scheme he devised later became standard on all RAF fighters.

His revolutionary idea of photography from unarmed, high-speed, high-flying aircraft was strongly resisted by most of the so-called experts. But it was soon adapted by the RAF's famed Photo Reconnaissance Unit which had grown from Cotton's tiny group.

"RAF Photographic Intelligence began through the pressure, persistence and enterprise of Sidney Cotton," wrote the post-war London *Times*.

Cotton's Australian individualism made him refuse to be hamstrung by bureaucracy. It led him to espouse the cause of the blockaded people of Hyderabad in 1948. Purchasing a fleet of cargo aircraft – converted Lancaster bombers – he ran his own mini-airlift. Ignoring government disapproval he carried arms, food and desperately needed medical supplies to the eighteen million starving people surrounded by the aggressive might of India.

When Hyderabad tragically fell, Cotton was in Karachi negotiating with the Pakistani government. His actions had made him many enemies in high places. Through a faithful Moslem servant, he learned that an attempt was to be made on his life that evening.

In typical swashbuckling fashion, he made his escape in style. He threw a huge party to which he invited Pakistani government officials and military officers, including those he knew would benefit most by his "accidental death". Later, when the party was in full swing, Cotton and two comrades slipped out quietly by a side door and drove to the airport. He managed to con a friendly customs official into letting them depart on an urgent business flight. Three days later he was in London.

To lend an air of official consternation to the whole airlift affair, the British government charged Sidney Cotton for breaches of the 1876 *Customs Act*. Though called a gun runner and adventurer at the ensuing trial, he was merely fined a paltry £200 and judged guilty of a technical offence only.

It was hinted years later that Sir Winston Churchill, then leading Her Majesty's Opposition, had personally expressed the wish that the court deal as leniently as possible with the adventurous Australian.

In 1956, following the Suez disaster, he again hit the headlines, when he turned his efforts into trying to bring to the British government a better understanding of Arab problems. He later negotiated with Prime Minister Harold Macmillan and his ministers on behalf of King Ibn Saud and other leaders of the oil-rich Middle Eastern states.

Cotton's talents and enthusiasm took him all over the

world. His life was as full of excitement as it was of incident. He was just as much at home with the seal hunters of Newfoundland as with the politicians, statesmen and members of royalty he so frequently met.

In 1969 he wrote of his wish to return with his family to the country of his birth. It was not to be. A few months later Sidney Cotton, Queensland airman-adventurer-inventor, who had helped win the war with a camera, was dead.

In a glowing obituary the London *Times* said:

> Cotton was one of the most remarkable men of his generation . . . He did not get as much credit as he deserved for he was constitutionally incapable of using "channels", was always cutting corners, and treading on toes to get his revolutionary ideas accepted, and had the annoying habit of proving experts wrong. These are not the qualities which endear one to a service superior in wartime. As a result he was frequently at odds with the authorities with whom he came in contact. They in turn did not love him more for being so often one jump ahead of them, for putting up ideas which they initially rejected but were ultimately obliged to adopt.
>
> His Hyderabad arms airlift was a fantastic operation, carried out in the teeth of every sort of opposition — political, bureaucratic and technical — which only somebody with Cotton's determination and genius for improvisation could have achieved.
>
> He leaves a wife and two children and a record of ruggedly individualistic, superbly unconventional behaviour, second only to his reputation for courage and resourcefulness.

His character was probably best personified by something he often told his friends: "About 80 per cent of my time was devoted to fighting the bone-heads in the Air Ministry. So only the remaining 20 per cent was left to me to perfect the Unit — and fight the Germans!"

14
Fastest Around
the World

This is the story of an Australian pilot who was determined to break an around-the-world record. It is not set in the great record-breaking era between the two World Wars; it took place in 1975. Nevertheless, the dramatic first attempt, ending in near-disaster over Canada, and the subsequent five-day non-stop flight which broke the record, had all the frustration, nerve-racking suspense and excitement of the early record attempts.

It is a story that I am fortunate to be able to tell first hand, as I was lucky enough to be in the cockpit of Denys Dalton's Beechcraft *Duke* when it circled the world from Brisbane to Brisbane.

It is possible that this flight will be the last major record-breaking effort by a propeller-driven Australian aircraft for, with the world's growing shortage of fossil fuels and the increasing need to conserve fuel, aircraft operators will be loath to squander thousands of precious litres chasing a record, even if they could afford the skyrocketing cost.

The kerosene-burning jets may still race the clock for a few years to come, but we are at the end of the era of the growling pistons with their flashing propellers, circling the earth on the heels of Wiley Post and Howard Hughes going for the "big one" — fastest around the world.

Denys Dalton was born in England in 1918. As a young boy he was fascinated by aircraft and during his school years at Beaumont College he closely followed the flights of the pioneers and record breakers — he was particularly entranced by the flights of Amy Johnson and her husband Jim Mollison.

Having decided to learn to fly, it was only a matter of choosing the best way to achieve his goal. By the time he finished school, the clouds of war were gathering over Europe and Britain was slowly waking to the need to expand her small peacetime air force.

Denys was one of hundreds who were accepted by the Royal Air Force for their Volunteer Reserve training system in 1938.

His first taste of active duty came in 1939 when he was one of a small group of RAF pilots sent to Finland by Prime Minister Neville Chamberlain when that tiny nation was fighting for its existence against the might of Russia.

The Finns appealed to England for help. They were particularly short of pilots and, not wishing to provoke a diplomatic situation with Russia, the British government decided against sending official military aid. Instead they called for volunteers from the RAFVR to go out as civilians and fly for beleaguered Finland.

Thus Denys Dalton went to war flying an outdated Bristol Bulldog biplane of the Finnish Air Force against the modern Polikarpov I-16 monoplane fighters and Illyushin bombers of the Russian Air Force. Finland's 116 aircraft, most of them obsolete, fought the Russian force of over 1000 aircraft to a standstill. It was not until February 1940, when the Russians had increased their force to 2000 aircraft, that Finland finally accepted Soviet surrender terms. By this time the English pilots had returned to the RAF and were defending England against the Luftwaffe.

Denys flew Hurricanes, then Spitfires. He had a close escape when, shot down over the English Channel, he force-landed in the water. His Spitfire nosed in on hitting the waves and he was catapulted out of the cockpit into the sea from where he was picked up by an air/sea rescue launch.

Later in the war he was posted to Australia and flew

with No. 54 Squadron in defence of Darwin. It began his long love affair with Australia and in 1946, when he was demobbed in England, he decided to move to Australia.

Rather than emigrate by sea, he chose to fly out and try to establish himself in Australia's post-war general aviation business. He bought a war-surplus Percival Proctor for £800. The single-engined, four-seat communications aircraft seemed an ideal choice, not only for the 20 000-kilometre flight, but also for his planned air taxi service.

The long, slow flight to Australia set no speed records but was an invaluable first taste of the problems of long-distance international flights. In particular, he became aware of the frustrations of bureaucratic red tape and the mountains of paperwork needed to get through the countries en route.

Once settled in Australia, he started Albury Air Taxis. They were tough days for commercial aviation, made tougher by the lack of interest shown by the government of the day. Denys eventually sold out and joined Australian National Airlines, flying DC 4 airliners.

In 1951 he decided on a break from aviation. With his Australian wife Norma he started a small, outdoor barbecue restaurant on a piece of bushland they purchased at a quiet weekend resort on the Queensland coast — the devotees of surfing who drove down the dusty track from Brisbane reckoned the section of coast was a real "surfer's paradise"!

In fact, it was these same surf addicts who made up the bulk of his trade. Under a tin roof, over a coke-fuelled grill, Denys and Norma fed them a huge steak and "all the spaghetti you can eat" . . . for 10 shillings! "The Barbecue" soon became the coast's best-known eating place and as Surfers Paradise grew, so did the restaurant.

By the late 1960s, the "El Rancho" barbecue was serving as many as 1000 steaks on a busy night. The open bush shed had grown into a huge restaurant and the dusty, bushland site had become a busy corner of downtown Surfers Paradise.

Night after night Denys and Norma ran the establishment with the same personal involvement: she managing the huge dining room and he sweating over the steak-covered grills.

But the passion for flying had not diminished. When there was a quiet period, the two would get away from it all in the Beechcraft Bonanza Denys had purchased in America. Rather than having the aircraft delivered by sea, he had flown it home across the Pacific. The Bonanza was followed by a twin-engined Travelair which enabled them to make a number of international flights to Europe, North America, and around the Pacific.

In 1969 he entered the England-Australia Air Race held to commemorate the fiftieth anniversary of the first flight to Australia made by the Smith brothers in their Vickers Vimy.

Denys made good time as far as Singapore, then was forced to drop out of the race. Where most entries had a two-man crew he had elected to do the flight on his own — sheer exhaustion forced him to give up in the final stages of the race. From this experience he learnt a vital lesson. For safe, long-distance air racing you need two pilots.

While visiting the Philippines in the same year, he saw a plaque bearing the names of two American flyers who had previously set a new record for the around-the-world flight. It started him thinking. Since the earliest days of flying, pilots had taken up the challenge of speed: either all-out records over a short course in specially designed speedsters or fastest point-to-point over long courses. Since 1927, when the United States Army's Douglas biplanes first circled the earth in 175 days, the around-the-world record had been the ultimate.

This was the record he wanted. His thirty years of flying and numerous international light-aircraft flights provided the bank of piloting experience needed for the attempt;

however, the problem was to find an aircraft with a high enough cruising speed. From a few quick calculations it was obvious that the Travelair was not fast enough and that he would have to lay his hands on an aircraft that could manage another 100 kph.

It was four years before he found it. His hope for the re-cord came in the shape of a sleek, twin-engined Beechcraft Duke which he named *The Duke of Broadbeach*. Equipped with turbo-charged, 380-horsepower piston engines it had a cruising speed of 380 kph. Fully pressurised, it had the added advantage of being able to cruise at 21 000 feet, above much of the bad weather.

As a warm-up for the big one, Denys decided to make an attempt on the Australia-England piston-aircraft record. His problem of finding a suitably experienced co-pilot was solved when an ex-Hungarian Air Force pilot offered to join him. John Bally, a Department of Transport Examiner of Airmen, had decided to make his first trip home since escaping from Hungary during the Communist takeover following the Second World War. This seemed an exciting way of reaching Europe.

Exciting it was. They left Brisbane on 21 October 1973 in clear weather, but by the time they had reached Darwin for refuelling the weather had turned bad. As they climbed out over the Timor Sea they were surrounded by violent tropical thunderstorms.

Despite unco-operative weather all the way to Pakistan, they made good time. When they touched down at London's Gatwick Airport the pair had set a new record of 51 hours 14 minutes and 25 seconds for the 18 500 kilometre flight. There was no doubt the Duke was fast enough to take out the world record; providing, that was, that the attempt didn't get bogged down in red tape at the refuelling stops. (Denys and John had experienced real problems getting fast refuelling turnarounds in India and the Middle East.) It was becoming obvious that, even if the plane performed correctly and the weather was favour-

able, the record could still be lost to time-wasting bureaucracy at the refuelling stops.

It took eighteen months of meticulous planning to organise the record attempt. Arrangements had to be made
with the Fédération Aéronautique Internationale in Paris
(the official body governing air racing) to have FAI officials at each of the planned landing points. Refuelling was
organised to be available the moment the Duke landed.
Customs, health and payment of landing fees had to be arranged. The Australian Department of Transport spent
months organising diplomatic and flight clearances. Maps,
radio navigation charts, flight plans, fuel computations, in-
flight rations, safety equipment . . . the preparations
seemed endless.

The Duke's passenger seats were removed and replaced with specially constructed fuel tanks, boosting the
aircraft's range to allow a sufficient safety margin for the
long, overwater legs – the 4000 kilometres from Honolulu
to San Jose, California, was the longest.

With John Bally unavailable for this flight, Denys had
asked Keith Carmody, President of the Royal Queensland
Aero Club, if he would like to share the cockpit. Keith,
himself a keen international flyer, jumped at the chance.

They left Brisbane in the early hours of 7 April 1975. All
went well across the Pacific. Following refuelling stops at
Tarawa Island, Honolulu and San Jose, the airmen were
well ahead of the record. They crossed North America and
refuelled at Toronto.

The next leg took them east to Gander on the Atlantic
coast. Climbing out of Toronto, they had just reached
cruising height when it happened: there was a brittle, me-
tallic clash followed by a total loss of power from the port
engine – a complete mechanical failure. Quickly they
feathered the propeller to reduce drag on the dead engine.

Within seconds it became apparent that with the heavy
load of fuel, the aircraft would not hold height on the remaining engine. They were in a steady powered descent.

A quick check of the charts showed the Royal Canadian Air Force base of Trenton lay ahead. It was just within range. They alerted the authorities and limped in to a safe landing; they had just enough range to make it.

Had the failure occurred at a similar stage of flight after take-off on the next leg, they would have come down in the Atlantic. It was a sobering thought for both pilots as they later inspected the failed engine. A cylinder had let go from the engine crankcase – a catastrophic breakdown.

Following a complete engine change, there was no chance of making the record, so the disappointed men made a leisurely flight across the Atlantic. From London they decided to salvage something from the ruins of the world flight: at least they could try for the England-Australia record on the way home.

Again they were dogged by bad luck. They were setting a cracking pace and were two hours out from Singapore when oil was seen escaping all over the starboard engine cowling. With the pressure falling alarmingly, they had no option but to shut down the ailing engine. Luckily, with most of the fuel already consumed on this leg, the Duke was relatively light and they had no problem carrying on to Singapore; in fact, they were still able to beat the existing London-Singapore record despite flying the last 650 kilometres on one engine.

A careful analysis of the remaining oil in the engine's sump disclosed that when the oil tank had been topped-up in Dubai the refueller had put in a substance more resembling treacle than aviation motor oil. Mixed with the engine's oil, it had caused the oil seals to blow out. It may have been a deliberate act to sell a few quarts of oil by a refueller who did not have the correct type (paradoxically, oil was extremely hard to come by in the Middle East) or just a careless mistake. Denys will never know, but either way it could have cost the men their lives. He made a decision right then: on the next attempt he or his partner would personally put in every drop of petrol and dribble of oil during the flight. With the rush for rapid turnarounds, he could not afford the dangers inherent with unskilled or unscrupulous refuellers looking after the job.

Despite the trauma of two failed engines, not to mention the cost so far incurred, Denys Dalton was already mentally organising another attempt. Shortly after his return to Brisbane, I met Denys on one of his frequent visits to Aviation House. We were having lunch together and discussing his next record attempt. I had earlier confided in John Bally that I would have given my eye-teeth to have made the earlier flight to London and wondered if Denys had anyone in mind for his latest venture.

Out of the blue, Denys said with a grin: "I hear you would like to come and dice with death with me."

I somewhat flippantly replied that I heard he was stopping over in London to refuel and as I hadn't seen my brother there for ten years I couldn't think of a better way of doing it. "Well, that's settled then," he replied.

Having written for some years about the early pioneer record breakers of aviation, it seemed a once-in-a-lifetime chance to experience in a small way a little of the rigours and excitement of record chasing. Although I could not match Denys' international flying experience I had flown over much of Europe and North America as a pilot with the RAF and later the RCAF and had made one Atlantic crossing.

Three months of intensive re-planning went into the second around-the-world attempt. One major alteration was made to the Duke's auxiliary fuel tank system: in view of the Canadian experience, a fuel-dump system was installed. If an emergency arose we could dump the excess fuel from the cabin tanks in a matter of a minute or so, which would enable the aircraft to keep flying on one engine should the need occur again.

Take-off was planned for 5 a.m. on 19 July 1975 from Brisbane's Eagle Farm Airport. The 39 419-kilometre route included eleven refuelling stops. One hour had been allowed at each to complete the mountain of formal paperwork, submit flightplan details, obtain up-to-the-minute weather information, and fill to brimming the Duke's six fuel tanks. Every second wasted on the ground was precious – the total time elapsed from leaving the ground at Brisbane until our return back overhead would count in arriving at the final average speed. No matter how fast we flew, the record could easily be lost on the ground if turnarounds took too long.

Denys had planned a target time of just under 118 hours, allowing for prevailing winds. It would mean an average speed of 335 kph – fast enough to break the record with a ten-hour margin to spare for any unexpected delays.

It was bitterly cold and pitch dark as we farewelled our families and climbed on board VH-TKE. To get into the pilots' seats was an ordeal in itself. We had to climb in through the Duke's rear cabin door, wriggle feet-first up and along the huge cabin fuel tanks with our noses brushing the cabin roof, and then slither down into the seats, making sure that our lambswool "ugg boots" did not displace a vital switch or control.

The engines had been warmed and checked, pre-take-off vital actions were completed, and everything was ready. Right on time, Brisbane Tower came up with take-off clearance; their terse, official instructions ended with a warm good-luck message.

The Duke's landing lights picked up ghostly ribbons of mist as Denys opened up to full power and the aircraft slowly accelerated down the long runway. In the cold, dense air, the heavily laden Beechcraft reached flying speed surprisingly quickly. Almost imperceptibly, Denys eased back on the control column. Immediately the rumbling of the wheels stopped as they left the runway, to be replaced by the whine of the electric motors folding the gear up into the aircraft.

It took a little while for the Duke to accelerate to climbing speed and start gaining a significant amount of height.

This was the critical period when a loss of power on either engine would be disastrous. As the airspeed needle reached 190 kph the Duke settled into a slow but steady climb.

Once 3000 feet had been gained there was enough height to cope with a sudden engine failure and sufficient time to dump the cabin fuel. Until then there would be no hope of staying airborne. Although we never discussed it, you could almost cut the tension with a knife during the first few minutes of each take-off. Once the Duke was up and climbing with engines singing sweetly was always the time for cheerful bantering.

It took forty minutes to reach the initial 18 000 feet cruising level, and as soon as we levelled off Denys throttled back to maximum cruising power. We had already switched to the cabin tanks – a complicated process involving operating fuel cocks and pump switches in a strict order. As one pilot went through the routine, the other carefully monitored his actions.

We were both aware of the need for careful and precise checks and procedures throughout the flight – particularly during the critical take-off, climb, descent and landing phases. One small omission or error could be fatal, and as the flight progressed we knew that fatigue was inevitable. Thus we had decided that both pilots must be on duty during these critical times throughout the flight; any sleeping would only be during the long cruising stages.

As the sun came up we were well out over the Pacific and it was time for our first meal. Norma Dalton had prepared and packaged all our meals for the flight. We would not afford the time to try to eat during stopovers, let alone risk the chance of picking up a stomach wog during our Middle East and Asian stops.

Our first meal was to be our only hot one: sausages and bacon cunningly stored in a large thermos flask. With the rolls and cheese we found a note from Norma wishing us an enjoyable breakfast – she had thought of everything.

Locked away in the Duke's ice-cold nose locker were all the meals for the next five days, each carefully labelled and each containing a message from Denys' wife. As the flight progressed, her messages of encouragement became increasingly important to our morale, and we looked forward to those tenuous links with home.

We expected to take ten hours to reach our first landing point on miniscule Tarawa Island. Once the radio compass was out of range of Brisbane's ABQ transmitter, we flew by dead reckoning. Four hours out we should pass close by a small coral reef – if we were more than a few kilometres off track we would miss it.

The reef came up on the horizon a few minutes early: we were on track and ahead of time. It was time for a minor celebration, so out came the plug-in water heater and within minutes we had hot coffee. If any one item of equipment could be singled out as absolutely vital to the success of the flight it would have to be the specially constructed water heater. With both of us normally heavy smokers, but unable to indulge in our habit because of the cabin fuel tanks, we resorted to endless cups of coffee as the flight progressed. Luckily the Duke was equipped with special cockpit relief tubes to combat the problems associated with constant drinking!

The reef-encircled island of Tarawa appeared ten minutes ahead of time. The coral was still littered with the rusting hulks of landing craft, reminding us of the terrible battle that took place during the Second World War – the US Marines suffered dreadful casualties before gaining control of the tiny island with its vital airstrip.

As was the planned routine for each of our eleven stops, Denys took off at a steady trot to handle the official formalities while I refuelled the Duke. The cabin tanks were a particular worry – having to be filled in strict rotation and ensuring every available litre of space was filled, yet not allowing a drop to overflow. Spilt fuel in the cabin would mean time-consuming drying-out and airing: a fuselage full of high-octane fumes would have been a virtual flying bomb.

A quick dash for a refreshing wash and we were airborne after only thirty-three minutes on the ground. Within a couple of hours I was to regret the wash. Somehow I must have picked up bacteria from the local water while splashing my face for, as we headed for Honolulu, I was suffering a Pacific version of "Delhi Belly". It was to stay around until we reached the Middle East — the place you would expect to pick it up, not lose it!

The flight to Honolulu went without a hitch. Denys dodged the line of violent storms which, as expected, sat along the intertropical front. The pitch-black night made it easy to pick out the lightning-filled cells and we gave them a wide berth.

The only problem was the after-sunset cold. Unfortunately the Duke's cockpit heater had packed up the first time we had switched it on after we left Brisbane. At our cruising level the outside temperature was near freezing, but by day the aircraft's interior was warmed by the sun. However, with the Pacific night it dropped dramatically. Luckily we had brought along woollen gloves and hats as well as insulated flying jackets — just in case. The four dollars spent at the Disposal Store had been an invaluable investment: chilled hands and heads could well have stopped the attempt. It was still very cold at night, but bearable.

Our course to Hawaii was not far south of that flown by Amelia Earhart and Fred Noonan thirty-eight years earlier, when they took off from New Guinea on the Pacific sector of their attempt at the same record. They vanished without trace near Howland Island. Charles Ulm and his crew had also disappeared west of Honolulu attempting a record in the other direction. As the Duke sped on eastwards over the vast ocean, who knows if we passed close to the final resting place of those great pioneers?

It was early morning when TKE touched down at

Honolulu's International Airport. As one might expect very early on a Sunday morning, things were quiet. No one gets up that early on a Sunday morning unless they have to and that turned out to be our first major problem.

Despite Denys' careful planning there was no one to be seen at the light-aircraft parking area. No officials and more importantly no fuel truck. Something had gone wrong. After a few frustrating minutes calling the tower on the aircraft's radio, the airport officials finally arrived. But still no fuel. Forty minutes passed before a tanker commanded by a bleary-eyed driver arrived on the scene.

Understandably Denys was furious. The driver lamely explained that he had overslept and anyway, he wasn't all that late! To cap it all, the Duke's tanks were only half full when the fuelling truck ran dry. He had forgotten to fill up the previous night. Another thirty minutes went by before he returned to complete the job.

When we taxied out again we had been an hour and forty minutes on the ground. In the twenty-four hours since leaving Brisbane we had gained twenty minutes on our schedule during the 7800 kilometres to Hawaii; as we took off for the United States we were twenty minutes behind due to one man's laziness.

For the first time on the flight I flew from the command seat while Denys monitored. We took off towards Diamond Head, slowly climbing out along the still-deserted beaches. Turning right to avoid the peak our sluggish aircraft could not outclimb, we set our heading for the 4000-kilometre overwater leg to San Jose, California. As the islands slipped astern, Denys reached over and switched on the weather radar, but instead of the comforting sweep of the scanner on the green screen we saw nothing but our own anxious reflections in the darkened glass. The radar had failed, and what was worse was the knowledge that we could not afford the precious time to have it repaired on this flight. To remove, test and repair the equipment could

take many hours — even if we could find a company prepared to meet us at our odd arrival times.

The flight would have to be completed without it. This
meant that we must either avoid storm clouds or take a
chance that we could punch our way through without entering a storm cell or heavy turbulence. The turbulence
was a particular problem because, with the massive fuel
load on board during the early hours of each leg, the
aircraft's ability to withstand the punishment imposed on
the airframe by pounding turbulence was greatly reduced.
For at least five or six hours we must avoid it like the
plague.

Halfway to San Jose, when far out of radio range and
flying purely by dead reckoning, we had a pleasant inter-
lude. A United States Air Force jet transport *Mac 03*
passed well above us. We could see his white contrails way
above, called him up on the radio, and for a few minutes
chatted with the crew. They were just returning home
from Australia and had left Brisbane twelve hours after us.
How we envied his speed. We invited the crew to join us
for a drink next time they were in Brisbane. The captain
answered: "We'd love to. By the way, there are twenty-six
of us on board and it will be your shout!"

When we picked up our first bearing on San Francisco
Radio, the Duke was only 40 kilometres north of track.
Not bad, considering that we had been navigating "blind"
for over 2000 kilometres. As we headed for nearby San
Jose Airport, we had been on the go for thirty-six hours
and the insidious effects of lack of sleep were creeping up
on us. Apart from a doze or two in the cabin, neither Denys
nor I had been able to sleep.

San Jose was covered in low cloud, and as the Duke descended for an instrument approach the dulling effect of
tiredness became obvious for the first time. I experienced
great difficulty in getting the aircraft settled on the glide
path, and in fact overshot the airport. Though clear of

cloud, we were in no position to land and had to make a wide circle to reposition on final approach.

With the mass of lights and the crisscross of brightly illuminated freeways I had great difficulty in sighting the runway lights. Finally we picked them out and landed safely. Imagine my frustration – I had wasted ten precious minutes. I was particularly angry because I had specifically chosen this leg as San Jose had been my home for four years.

I had worked right alongside the airport and knew the area like the back of my hand. Still, things could have been worse, for we were still thirty-five minutes ahead of our planned time – which in turn put us well ahead of the record.

Waiting outside the darkened terminal was a small cluster of people – friends from ten years earlier who had kept a vigil until three in the morning to renew our old friendship. It was one of the most frustrating moments of the flight to have to carry out refuelling with no more than a moment or two to talk with them. Nevertheless, their thoughtful act gave us both the mental lift we needed after the long Pacific crossing.

A rapid, well-organised turnaround at San Jose helped pick up a few vital minutes. Thirty-five minutes after landing, we were speeding off again towards the heartland of America.

As the lights of San Francisco passed below, we turned slowly east to fly the great circle track direct to Toronto. Over most of the United States we would have the benefit of ground radar observing our flight path. The American controllers gave us every possible assistance – they obviously appreciated the vital importance of making the direct track available so as not to waste precious minutes.

Once Denys had completed the changeover to the cabin tanks, I was ordered back from the flight deck to catch some sleep in the rest area. Denys was well aware that I was still suffering the discomfort of "Tarawa Tummy" and insisted that he was not in the least tired and that if necessary he could stay awake on his own until London. An exaggeration, perhaps, but an example of his unselfish concern; he was just as tired as I was, having dozed off only a couple of times during the Pacific crossing.

The rest area was a narrow mattress positioned along the top of a cabin fuel tank. By any standards it was cramped and uncomfortable. Beneath was the gurgling, echoing fuel and above was the wind-swept cabin ceiling; and yet, at that moment, it was the most luxurious and comfortable bed in the world. For the next few hours I slept the sleep of the dead. Up front my companion fought tiredness and an increasing headwind as he headed over the foothills of the Rocky Mountains.

As dawn broke, he was concerned to see an endless wall of storm clouds on the horizon. Ground control confirmed that a violent tornado was sweeping down across the central United States and lay directly in the Duke's path. As Denys headed on, hoping the storm's rapid movement would move it south of our path, he cursed the failed radar − this was just the time its vital scanning was needed to pick the storm centres out of the expanse of grey cloud that loomed ahead.

Unable to climb above the wall, he sadly turned north at right angles to the flight path. This was the time that two pairs of eyes were needed and the experience of two pilots could best determine the safest yet fastest way of getting past the storms. He called me out of my sleep to join him up front.

Denys skirted the line of towering storm clouds searching for a safe corridor. Several times he headed for likely looking gaps only to see them disappear as the rapidly moving clouds merged. Fifteen disconcerting minutes went by before a more permanent break appeared. As we headed into the valley between two massive heads of cloud, we watched anxiously for signs of them merging. If they came together we had no hope of climbing out of their turbulent, hail-filled centres as they soared at least 10 000 feet above our maximum cruising height. Our luck held, and ten minutes later the storm clouds were astern as we headed south-east to regain our track. We later learned that the storm left a trail of death and devastation over a number of mid-western States.

Thirty vital minutes had been lost during that storm diversion over Sioux Falls, Idaho. We were still ahead of the old record, but slipping back on our planned time. However, the magnificent organisation of Canadian officials and refuellers at our next two stops regained the lost time. With forty-five-minute turnarounds at Toronto and Gander, Newfoundland, we were back on schedule as we headed out over the grey Atlantic.

Once we had reached cruising level and Denys had monitored my selection of the long-range tanks, he snaked his way back to the fuel tank bed for a well-earned rest. It was fifty-four hours since we had left Brisbane and in that time he had not left the cockpit except for the mad forms-signing scramble at the refuelling stops. He had dozed occasionally while I was occupying the command seat, but had not had a worthwhile rest. He had the stamina of a man half his age but now wisely decided it was time to try and give body and mind a recharging rest. There was still a long way to go and past London was Europe and the Middle East, with their constricting air traffic procedures; and further on India — where anything could happen.

We crossed the Atlantic in darkness. The long hours were broken by routine position reports each thirty minutes and the answering voices from far-off land were welcome and reassuring. At times during periods of radio silence in the mid-Atlantic night one felt utterly alone and strangely detached from the rest of the world, and to while away the hours and remain alert was a challenge.

Throughout the flight, both Denys and I resorted to the professional pilot's strict routine of constantly monitoring the engines' instruments and between times working and reworking the navigation log. Another time-consuming chore was managing the Duke's fuel system. As each of the cabin tanks ran low, one of the two engines was switched to a new tank. The remaining engine was left to suck the last few litres of avgas from the dying tank. During those few minutes the pilot waited with hands poised over fuel cocks and pump switches for the first sign of the tank running dry. Then, as the fuel pressure gauge started to drop, accompanied by a loss of power on that engine, a flurry of hands switched the faltering engine over to the new tank. Only this way could we guarantee that we had used every precious drop of fuel in the cabin tanks. It was a process that required close attention and split-second timing so as not to lose a significant amount of power from the engine. As the flight progressed and we grew more tired, it placed continually increasing demands on our concentration.

With dawn we approached Ireland. The first grey light disclosed an unbroken carpet of altostratus cloud below. Denys rejoined me up front and unwrapped Norma's carefully labelled "day three" breakfast. Before we ate he read out her "Good Morning" message.

The meal was over and we were tidying away when the Duke's distance measuring equipment locked in. We were getting a reading much earlier than expected and if it was right we had picked up a roaring tailwind through the night. The readout remained steady and following some quick calculations Denys broke into a broad grin. We were forty-five minutes ahead of our planned time for the 3800-kilometre crossing and had averaged 35 kph better than expected.

Even the inevitable rain at London's Gatwick Airport could not dampen our excitement as we taxied in. We were halfway around the world and were still nearly eight hours ahead of the record. I had another cause for excitement: waiting on the tarmac was my brother Patrick whom I had not seen for ten years.

As I refuelled, we had a hectic family reunion. As the owner of Chelsea's "Pomegranates" restaurant, it was not surprising to find he had brought along a lunch fit for a king and a magnum of French champagne to wash it down. Unfortunately we just could not afford the time to eat, but loaded a huge dish of his "speciality" "Gravad Lax" — marinated raw salmon in a fabulous sauce — into the cockpit. And, of course, the champagne. They would be ideal for a victory celebration when we got home. After only forty-three minutes on the ground we took off on the ten-hour leg to Damascus.

"Victor Kilo Echo . . . permission to overfly Greece has been denied . . . you are to return to London . . ." the message from Frankfurt Radio blared from the aircraft's loudspeakers. For a moment there was stunned silence in the cockpit, then Denys reacted angrily to the incredible instruction.

"Frankfurt Radio, this is Victor Kilo Echo. There has to be some mistake. Please advise the Greek authorities that I have copies of the clearances to overfly Greece on board. We are continuing as planned until you confirm."

At this stage the aircraft was still an hour away from the edge of Greek airspace, heading towards a narrow corridor bordering on unco-operative Albania. Provided we remained in the corridor, we could carry on for another 300 kilometres before hitting the area commanded by Athens Control.

While we waited for further information from Frankfurt Radio, Denys and I considered our situation. There was no doubt the Greek authorities had approved our flight — we carried Australian Department of Transport approval covering the whole flight. The European sector had been meticulously arranged by DOT's London-based John Perry and there was no way that he would have neglected to check with Greece.

Our fear was that the controlling officers in Athens had mislaid or never received our flight authorisation. It could take them days to dig it up and in the meantime we would be forced to return to London and wait. With the problems of getting diplomatic approval to fly over Europe, there was no other route we could fly without weeks of preparation – if the Greeks still said no, the record was gone.

Ten nerve-racking minutes passed before the Frankfurt controller came on air again. In a voice tinged with sympathy he told us that Athens Control denied all knowledge of our approval and still refused to let us enter their airspace.

There was now a mere forty minutes' flight time between the aircraft and the wall of bureaucratic incompetence. There had to be an answer. Looking at his watch, Denys calculated the local time in London. It was mid-afternoon there. Was it possible that we could somehow raise John Perry at his city office?

"Frankfurt Radio, this is Victor Kilo Echo . . . could you please try and reach Mr John Perry at the Australian High Commissioner's office in London and advise him of the situation. Ask him to phone the Greek authorities."

It was a pretty tall order to ask an unknown controller in Germany. But when Denys advised him that we were trying for a world-record flight, he agreed to phone London.

For the next twenty minutes we headed for Greece. If the clearance was not forthcoming, it was all over unless we were prepared to chance a low-level dash across the Mediterranean. At wave-top height we would be no hazard to other aircraft, but if the Greeks picked us up on the radar all hell would break loose – and then the legal possibilities . . .! It didn't bear thinking about, but at that moment we were two tired, frustrated and angry pilots. We decided to cross that bridge when we got to it.

We never had to. Somehow the improbable network of communication worked. Our anonymous German controller reached John Perry, who in turn was able to contact the right man in Athens. We were ten minutes short of Greek control when the message came over the radio: "Victor Kilo Echo . . . disregard previous instructions . . . you are cleared to enter Athens Controlled Airspace at flight level One Eight Zero. Call Athens Control at 1610 Zulu.''

The tension was broken as we laughed and chattered. Why not? We were over halfway home and on the downhill run to down under.

Our gay mood was to be short lived, however. For some time we had been watching a towering cumulus cloud on the horizon. Initially it had seemed to lie to one side of the narrow air corridor we were tracking into Greece, but as we looked ahead we saw it had moved slowly eastwards and was now lying directly in our path. And, furthermore, it was rapidly building into a towering cumulonimbus cloud. Literally, as we watched, we could see its boiling top rise and spread out into the anchor formation which identifies a fully developed storm cloud. The solid column of cloud had turned from white into a dirty, grey-green mass announcing the intense turbulence and hail within its walls.

Flanked by two developing companions, the cloud mass had spread right across the corridor and rose at least 30 000 feet above us. To the west further storms were strung out like a line of sentinels. Our only way around lay over Albania, and that was a no-go area: the Albanians not only refused passage to non-vital aircraft, but we had also been strongly cautioned not to stray into their airspace. They policed the corridor on radar and unauthorised penetration of their jealously guarded airspace would most likely lead to interception by their MiG jet fighters. The diplomatic ramifications of such an action would be shattering.

Denys and I held a quick cockpit conference. We could not outclimb the storm, nor was there any way around. It could take hours for the line of thunderheads to pass through, and anyway we had no diplomatic clearances to land in that area, let alone the time and the possibility of losing the record. We decided to fly through.

As the wall of cloud approached, Denys reduced speed to that recommended for turbulence penetration – to lessen the stress imposed on the Duke's airframe by the turbulence we would encounter. I made a last-minute check that there was no loose equipment in the cockpit likely to be flung around, and we tightened our restraining harness until we were anchored in our seats.

In the next few minutes all hell broke loose. It seemed as though giant hands had grabbed our little aircraft and were trying to shake the life out of it. Denys could do little other than hold a level attitude on the artificial horizon — the instrument which related the Duke's attitude to the earth's horizon. The airspeed indicator, altimeter, vertical speed indicator and compass needles went haywire — one second our speed showed as 250 knots and the next as 100. The noise of rain and hail hitting the airframe was deafening — our stomachs were in our mouths one moment and the next they were in our boots. For the first time I really wondered what I was doing on this mad escapade when I could be quietly relaxing at home.

It only lasted minutes, but it seemed an eternity. Then, as suddenly as we had entered, we broke out into sunshine and ahead were clear skies and the Mediterranean. We were through, but at a price: the Duke's windscreen was cracked from top to bottom and a fine trail of fuel was siphoning out of the starboard engine fuel tank. What we didn't know until hours later at Dubai was that the hail had punched a fist-sized hole right through the aircraft's nose.

Taking stock of the situation, Denys reset the fuel system so as to run down the leaking tank as quickly as possible; the windscreen would have to wait until we reached home. Within minutes the fuel had ceased spraying overboard. It was obvious that the leak was high in the system, close to the filler neck; for the rest of the flight we would be unable to fully utilise its capacity. Shortly afterwards one of the aircraft's two generators and the distance measuring equipment also packed up, further legacies of the storm.

Under Greek control we were heading east-south-east

across the sea for Damascus. Even though they had been talked into letting us through their airspace, the controllers were decidedly unco-operative: rather than allow us to follow our flight planned — and approved — direct path, they forced Denys to swing far to the south on a long diversion which wasted forty precious minutes.

It was approaching midnight as we joined the circuit for our Damascus landing. Denys had been at the controls throughout the ten incident-filled hours since we had left London seemingly an age ago. As he levelled off on the downwind landing leg, Damascus Tower dropped a bombshell. "Victor Kilo Echo . . . You are advised that there is no aviation gasoline available at Damascus. Advise your intentions . . ."

We were stunned. So much for all the careful planning. We held over the aerodrome while we checked our fuel reserves. We could make Beirut.

"Damascus Tower . . . is there any fuel at Beirut?"

"Victor Kilo Echo . . . we are not sure . . . there might be some."

An hour later we landed at Lebanon's troubled capital. For the third time on that problem leg from London, our luck held good.

We nearly came to grief on take-off. High mountains rise to the east of the city. It was pitch black as we struggled for height in the hot night air and we had been holding our assigned heading for some minutes when the controller called to check our compass. According to his radar we were way off course. Only then did we find that the switch that brings electrical power to the navigational equipment had been knocked off. Somehow as we clambered down into the cockpit seats in Beirut's darkness, an ill-placed foot or arm had turned it off. It was the sort of mistake one would normally have picked up immediately, but coming on top of the drama of the previous ten hours (compounded by three days of non-stop flying) it was a salutary warning that fatigue was catching up. We turned it on and quickly corrected our heading.

The 2000 kilometres to Dubai were uneventful and we landed in the mud-coloured, dusty city in the heat of mid-morning. It was then that a daylight inspection of the air-craft disclosed the hail-damaged nose. Helpful British Airways engineers bandaged the punctured nose with metal tape that would have to do until we reached Brisbane.

The temperature had soared to 48^0 C when we taxied out for take-off at the traffic crossroad city on the Arabian Gulf. Thus I needed nearly every metre of the huge run-way to get airborne. On our track to Madras a range of rag-ged mountains rose to 3300 metres and our flight path was through a pass 1000 metres above sea level. At full-climb power we just managed to reach our minimum safe height as we entered the pass 50 kilometres after leaving Dubai.

Across the Arabian Sea Denys finally went down the back end and caught a few hours of well-deserved sleep: he had been up front non-stop since leaving London eighteen hours earlier.

The weather experienced on the way to India is best de-scribed as filthy. Clouds and thunderstorms necessitated continual heading changes. Unable to climb above the weather, which made long-range radio contact virtually impossible, I was forced to relay position reports via other higher-flying aircraft.

It was a Qantas 747 en route to Singapore which eventu-ally took on a shepherding role as we crossed the sea. For several hours the crew relayed messages, passed weather observations, and encouraged us as they caught up to, passed high over, and finally flew out of, range of the Duke's radio.

One of the Qantas' captain's last messages was a prom-ise that on his arrival in Singapore he woud call my wife Susan in Australia with the news that TKE and her crew were still airborne and that all was well. His gesture was a great morale booster for us both, and later generated great excitement back in Brisbane when Susan received his call in the early hours of the morning.

Refuelling at Madras was an experience akin to a Gilbert and Sullivan comedy, but at the time it was no laughing matter. Denys literally ran from office to office attempting to speed up the process of obtaining the endless signatures needed for onwards flight clearance. He was armed with a fistful of dollars to "keep the wheels rolling". Bureaucrats are painfully slow in India. Terribly polite, mind you, but the word "speed" does not exist in their vocabulary – that is, until they happen to catch sight of a cash incentive. Just imagine the frustration of a dozen different forms to be filled out, always in triplicate (often in six copies), and an organisation that possesses no carbon paper!

While Denys battled the half-century-out-of-date system I was battling a surging crowd of beggars, tarmac attendants and curious bystanders who had appeared as if by magic in the middle of the night.

During the chaos around the aircraft I had to stop refuelling at least a dozen times to remove uninvited "guests" from the aircraft. Twice after I had replaced fuel-tank caps, deft hands removed them, then were held out palms upwards requesting a fee to replace them. Army personnel stood by and watched, either unable or not caring to control the crowd.

The final blow came when Denys returned to the aircraft and went to pay the refuelling agent. He disclaimed all knowledge of any prior arrangements and flatly refused to honour Denys' Indian Oil fuel carnet. Instead he demanded cash – over $600 for the 1000 litres we had taken. That worked out at three times the going price! It was daylight robbery and everyone knew it, but the refuellers also knew we were after a record and would not wait until morning when management came on duty.

There was no option but to pay if we wished to leave

Madras. It took the last of our cash fund to meet the bill. We had just started up the engines when they added insult to injury. The head refueller came running back with a band of his countless assistants who grouped in front of the aircraft while the leader clambered up on the rear of the wing. Denys opened the window and a heated conversation followed. The man insisted that Denys had short-changed him by $10 and he would not move his men until the sum was paid.

It was hopeless to argue. Between us we dug up a couple of Australian dollars, a pound note, and an American dollar. Denys rolled the notes together and showed them to the Indian but refused to pass them out until he moved his human barrier. The refuelling agent waved the mob away and then reached forward. Denys tossed the notes out of the window where the propeller slipstream blew them into the crowd herded behind the aircraft. As we moved away, I caught a final glimpse of scores of turbanned bodies diving for the fluttering notes.

As we taxied out to the runway we were furious at our treatment in Madras. Only when the flight was a relaxed memory could we comprehend and understand the desperate poverty of a nation which could produce such human behaviour. To India's millions of starving poor we must have appeared like millionaires who wouldn't miss the money. If we and our families were starving in the streets, would we have acted differently?

During the eight-hour flight to Singapore I noticed that Denys was looking unwell. Also his voice was giving out. He had been unable to obtain any water fit for drinking during our Indian stopover. Consequently we were down to the last few dregs in the cabin's ten-litre container. When this was finished, soon after leaving Madras, the insidious effects of dehydration began to show. A search of our cabin supplies revealed two small tins of chocolate custard that Norma Dalton had provided as a dessert for that evening's meal. They contained only a small amount of fluid, but it was enough to prevent the situation worsening over the last couple of hours of the flight to Singapore.

Seletar Airport appeared out of the early dawn mists that swirled over the island. Control refused to let us use the long runways at the International Airport, instead diverting us to Seletar, the smaller, ex-Royal Air Force airfield now used by general aviation aircraft.

This posed a real problem that nearly cost the record. We were restricted on take-off by having only 1730 metres of runway available. Combined with the sweltering heat, this put severe restrictions on the amount of fuel we could take on for the flight to Darwin. Our endurance and range were cut by a quarter.

As we left Singapore, we knew that if we encountered unforecast headwinds or delaying storms we could not reach Darwin. It was not our day – we met them both.

Abeam of Borneo, huge storms on the intertropical front drove Denys way off course. There seemed no way around them: neither by climbing nor descending to a few hundred metres over the sea could he find a way through. With the aircraft already suffering from the effects of the storm over Greece there was no way we could afford to risk the damaged nose and windscreen in another, similar storm. What made matters worse was the fact that these thunderstorms were hidden in a massive cloudbank that stretched from horizon to horizon. If our weather radar had not packed up over the Pacific we could have picked our way through, but as it was we were stymied.

It was then that we heard a Royal Australian Air Force transport aircraft calling Singapore Radio. It, too, was on its way to Darwin. We contacted the captain, who was sitting north of our position and above the worst of the weather, and he was able to guide us north over Borneo and talk Denys around the worst of the storms. But when we finally regained track heading for Timor we had lost an hour.

Even though the headwinds had abated, a quick check

of the remaining fuel showed that we would probably run out of petrol about ten minutes short of Darwin! To complicate the problem, there were only two possible landing places ahead on the islands where we might find fuel; however, they could not be reached before dark and neither had runway lighting.

All of a sudden came the shattering realisation that we could not carry on. The only suitable airport available was Macassar in the Indonesian Celebes Islands. That lay an hour away off our port wingtip, but an unannounced landing in Indonesia without the necessary approvals could spell disaster. Denys and I were both aware that English airwoman Sheila Scott had diverted to Macassar during the 1969 England-Australia Air Race and had been detained by the authorities for a week. Many stories had been told of other airmen receiving similar treatment when they inadvertently arrived unannounced at Indonesian airports. What made things worse was that the airport we were now forced to divert to was also a restricted military base.

Once again we checked and rechecked our fuel. It was no use. With a crestfallen shake of his head Denys turned for the Celebes. He wanted that record – he could almost taste success, for we were about ten hours ahead of the old one – but to carry on (hoping for a tailwind) would have verged on suicidal and we both knew it.

Denys raised Darwin on HF radio and told them the news, knowing they were powerless to help but at least ensuring those at home knew where we had landed – a message could take days from the Celebes. We headed away from Australia in silence. We had come so close. The disappointment was overwhelming; there were no words of consolation to fit that moment.

Macassar Tower, as we had expected, was surprised when our aircraft arrived unexpectedly in their area. The airfield seemed almost deserted as we taxied into the parking area alongside the control tower. By the time we opened the door armed military personnel were waiting alongside the Duke. Denys was escorted over to the nearby Commandant's Office while I was left at the aircraft with three soldiers. I noticed the refuelling compound and office about a hundred metres away and pointed towards it, indicating I wished to be taken there. I was escorted to the building and once inside was confronted by half a dozen desks, each manned by a grim-faced Indonesian. I went to the first and attempted to communicate in English and sign language that I wished to purchase fuel. I showed the disinterested official our Pertofina (Indonesian fuel company) credit card. After a few frustrating minutes he merely shook his head and pointed to the next desk in line. This was repeated from desk to desk. Eventually I was approached by an Army officer who had watched the charade and who told me in perfect English that the only fuel available would cost $3 for four litres in cash. He also pointed out that even with fuel we would not be able to leave until official approval came from Jakarta.

"How long will that take?" I asked.

"A week – possibly two," he calmly replied.

Aware that our cash was gone – thanks to the Madras incident – I decided to return and wait by the aircraft. It could take weeks to organise the funds from Australia. Minutes later another aircraft landed and taxied in alongside where I was sitting disconsolately. To my surprise I noticed it had an Australian registration. I was even more surprised when I found I recognised the pilot who climbed down out of the cockpit. I had met him just once, only weeks before, when he had visited me on business in Brisbane.

He walked over to me and then asked if we had any problem. In minutes I recounted the situation. He then told me he was working under contract to the Indonesian government and would see what he could do about the fuel situation. "They have plenty here," he said.

Ten minutes later he was back. The authorities had

agreed to sell him some but were adamant they would not put it into the Duke.

The only way out was to get them to fill his tanks then for both aircraft to taxi into one of the old wartime dispersal points in the surrounding jungle. There we could siphon his tanks and transfer the fuel to the Duke. As long as they didn't actually see us transfer the fuel, the Indonesians would not prevent us refuelling he said.

While all this was going on, Denys had been explaining to the authorities why we had arrived unannounced at their airport. With all hope of breaking the record gone, his concern was to prevent an unpleasant diplomatic wrangle and to try and get us away from Macassar as soon as possible. He had been able to convince the commandant that we had obtained diplomatic and air traffic clearances to overfly Indonesian territory and that our landing was due to a fuel emergency. Was it possible that if, and when, we could obtain fuel that the commandant would allow us to take off?'' he asked. The commandant indicated that he would call Jakarta.

Knowing we had no cash left to purchase fuel, the commandant probably thought that the matter of permission was purely academic.

Denys heard the Duke start up as I taxied away with the other aircraft. He wondered what was going on — probably I had been instructed to move the aircraft to some other parking space, he thought. For another hour he waited in the commandant's office.

The spot we had chosen to transfer the fuel was about 3 kilometres away amid dense jungle. The Japanese had built dozens of dispersal points and small hangars on the fringes of the airfield during the Second World War. As I followed the other aircraft along a rough track, I caught glimpses of waving women and children from a nearby village. Chickens and dogs scattered before us, frightened by the noise and we eventually stopped in a clearing by a Second World War hangar.

The transfer took two hours. All we had was a 200-litre drum and a small hand pump. Each stroke of the pump extracted half a litre of fuel into the drum. When the drum was full we rolled it alongside the Duke and repeated the laborious process to transfer the petrol into our aircraft. It was sweltering, and we worked in our underwear.

The last drumful was being transferred when a hilarious sight came into view. A small motor bike was approaching and on it was perched a dumpy Indonesian officer and riding pillion, towering over him, was Denys. The bike stopped long enough for Denys to hop off and then disappeared quickly back up the track with chickens flying in all directions.

"Well, when we can organise some cash to buy fuel I think they will let us leave," Denys called as he walked towards me. I then told him that we now had enough in the tanks to reach Darwin. Denys didn't react at all to the news. He was obviously still very depressed. It was then that I realised that he had not understood the significance of what I had said.

As I had been pumping fuel, I had mentally gone over our situation, taking into account the time we had been ahead of the old record when we left Singapore that morning, and the hours we had wasted at Macassar. I reckoned if we could get away then we could still beat the record. Not by the ten hours we had hoped for, but by at least two or three.

I quickly ran through the figures for Denys and suddenly he came alive again. "I had hoped for a ten-hour margin," he said, "but hell if we can go through all this and still beat it by ten minutes that will be really something."

We will never know whether we caught the controller napping or whether the commandant felt sorry for us, but a little while later as we taxied back alongside the control tower and headed for the runway rather than the parking lot, I called up for take-off clearance. I could see Denys almost freeze in anticipation of his answer. Quite unconcernedly the voice came over the radio: "Victor Kilo Echo . . . Macassar Tower clears you for take-off."

As Denys opened the throttles we turned the radio off. If the authorities changed their mind, we did not want to know about it. A minute later we were airborne, climbing over the ocean towards Darwin. We turned the radios back on and called Darwin. We heard no other calls from Macassar and when we reached Australia's northern gateway late that night we were still nearly three hours ahead.

Our turnaround took just twenty minutes, thanks to super-efficient controllers, refuellers and local aero club members who turned out in the middle of the night to feed and encourage us.

Denys had been at the controls non-stop for nearly twenty-four hours, so I took the first shift of the final leg to Brisbane. We hoped to gain an extra thirty minutes on the leg, but again the forecast tailwinds were not around. With Denys asleep up back, we crossed the continent over Mount Isa and headed past Longreach.

We were both exhausted. This was brought home with a start when suddenly one, then both, engines faltered and stopped – I had let the cabin tank run dry. A mad flurry of hands and selectors and within seconds both engines were purring smoothly again. From down the back end Denys, awakened from his sleep by the sudden silence, merely laughed. "Well, that sorted you out," he called. Shortly afterwards he took over while I caught some sleep.

"Victor Kilo Echo . . . Brisbane is closed due to fog." The message came just a few hours out from our destination – right to the last the elements were making things difficult. It was eventually decided that we would make a low sweep over the airport so that the official Fédération Aéronautique Internationale observer could formally time our arrival. Without this being done, our record would not be recognised by the world's air-racing body.

Until the last moment we hoped that the fog would burn off in time for us to land back at Brisbane, but it was not to be. As Denys lined up with the hangars that poked up in the swirling mist we were still unable to pick the runway.

At 8.04 a.m. Brisbane time, the Beechcraft Duke VH-TKE swept over Brisbane's control tower at 1500 feet and the official observer caught a glimpse of it through a break in the mist — a tough, exciting, and dramatic 122 hours and 40 minutes since it had lifted off from runway 04.

Our families and friends had gathered at Brisbane in the hope that we could land there. They now had a two-hour drive to Coolangatta airport where Denys had elected to land. "Norma will never forgive me if we land and she is not there," Denys confided as we headed for the Gold Coast. So for the next two hours we circled over the Gold Coast and Denys gave me an aerial commentary of his home town.

Suddenly we were no longer tired: the excitement of the record had given us a second wind. The traumas of the flight from London were forgotten as we laughed and joked away the waiting time. As Denys finally taxied his travel-scarred aircraft to its parking spot on Coolangatta airport, the tower controller called up: "I don't suppose we can expect to see you airborne this afternoon for a few practice circuits?"

"Not today," Denys replied, "but probably tomorrow."

Our flight earned not only the speed record around the world for piston-engined aircraft, but also the fastest time from London to Darwin; this despite the long delays we suffered. The Duke also beat the existing trans-Atlantic record, but it was not officially recognised as that leg had not been nominated for a record attempt before the flight.

For Denys Dalton, six years of planning and frustration had finally paid off. But records are there to be broken and their fame is a fleeting thing.

Three years after our flight, two American pilots set a new record. They were fortunate to have the assistance of the United States Air Force and were able to make most of their refuelling stops at USAF bases, thus cutting out all the red tape and saving hours of ground time. This made the big difference. But I wonder if, when it was all over, they maybe missed the satisfaction of overcoming the seemingly impossible problems that confronted Denys Dalton's record bid.

Bibliography

Affleck, Arthur. *The Wandering Years*. Croydon: Longmans, Green and Co., 1964.

Babington-Smith. Constance, *Evidence in Camera*. London: Chatto and Windus, 1968.

Barker, Ralph. *Verdict on a Lost Flyer*. London, George G. Harrap and Co. Ltd, 1969.

___. *Aviator Extraordinary*. London: Chatto and Windus, 1969.

Chichester, Sir Francis. *Solo to Sydney*. London: John Hamilton Ltd, 1930.

___. *Seaplane Solo*. London: Faber and Faber, 1932.

___.*The Lonely Sea and the Sky*. London: Pan Books, 1967.

Ellison, Norman. *Flying Matilda*. Sydney: Angus & Robertson, 1961.

Eustis, Nelson. *Australia's Greatest Air Race*. Adelaide: Seal Books Rigby, 1977.

Fysh, Sir Hudson. *Qantas Rising*. Sydney: Angus & Robertson, 1965.

Godwin, John. *Battling Parer*. Adelaide: Rigby, 1968.

Gunn, John. *The Defeat of Distance*. St Lucia: University of Queensland Press, 1985.

Gwynn-Jones, Terry. *Aviation's Magnificent Gamblers*. Sydney: Lansdowne Press, 1981.

___. *True Australian Air Stories*. Adelaide: Rigby, 1977.

___. *Heroic Australian Air Stories*. Adelaide: Rigby, 1981.

___. *Pioneer Aviator — The Remarkable Life of Lores*

Bonney. St Lucia: University of Queensland Press, 1988.

Joy, William. *The Aviators*. Sydney: Shakespeare Head Press, 1965.

Mackenzie, Roy. *Solo — The Bert Hinkler Story*. Brisbane: Jacaranda Press Pty Ltd, 1962.

Parer, Raymond. *Flight and Adventures of Parer and McIntosh*. Melbourne: J. Roy Stevens, 1921.

Rowe, Percy. *The Great Atlantic Air Race*. London: Angus & Robertson, 1977.

Thomas, Lowell. *Sir Hubert Wilkins*. Brisbane: The *Courier-Mail* Readers Book Club, 1963.

Index